Dr Melanie Fennell is an internationally recognized cognitive therapy practitioner and trainer. She is Director of an Advanced Cognitive Therapy course based at Oxford Cognitive Therapy Centre and Oxford University. She is a recognized expert in low self-esteem and has run workshops and presented papers at major international conferences.

COOPER, Professor of
norary NHS Consultant
nia nervosa and binge-
o help many thousands
n of the series is to help
and disorders to take
the latest techniques
h its specially tailored
any books in the Over-
Department of Health

19·01·10

1 0 MAR 2014

Other titles in the Overcoming series:

3-part self-help courses

Overcoming Anxiety Self-Help Course
Overcoming Bulimia Nervosa and Binge-Eating Self-Help Course

Single volume books

Overcoming Anger and Irritability
Overcoming Anorexia Nervosa
Overcoming Anxiety
Bulimia Nervosa and Binge-Eating
Overcoming Childhood Trauma
Overcoming Chronic Fatigue
Overcoming Chronic Pain
Overcoming Compulsive Gambling
Overcoming Depression
Overcoming Insomnia and Sleep Problems
Overcoming Low Self-Esteem
Overcoming Mood Swings
Overcoming Obsessive Compulsive Disorder
Overcoming Panic
Overcoming Relationship Problems
Overcoming Sexual Problems
Overcoming Social Anxiety and Shyness
Overcoming Traumatic Stress
Overcoming Weight Problems
Overcoming Your Smoking Habit

OVERCOMING
LOW SELF-ESTEEM
SELF-HELP COURSE

A 3-part programme based on Cognitive Behavioural Techniques

Part Two: Combating Self-Criticism and Enhancing Self-Acceptance

Melanie Fennell

ROBINSON
London

Constable & Robinson Ltd
3 The Lanchesters
162 Fulham Palace Road
London W6 9ER
www.overcoming.co.uk

First published in the UK by Robinson,
an imprint of Constable & Robinson Ltd 2006

Important Note
This book is not intended as a substitute for medical advice or treatment.
Any person with a condition requiring medical attention should consult
a qualified medical practitioner or suitable therapist.

ISBN 13: 978-1-84529-237-9 (Pack ISBN)
ISBN 10: 1-84529-237-5

ISBN 13: 978-1-84529-392-5 (Part One)
ISBN 10: 1-84529-392-4

ISBN 13: 978-1-84529-393-2 (Part Two)
ISBN 10: 1-84529-393-2

ISBN 13: 978-1-84529-394-9 (Part Three)
ISBN 10: 1-84529-394-0

3 5 7 9 10 8 6 4 2

Printed and bound in the EU

Contents

Introduction   vii

SECTION 1: Checking Out Anxious Predictions   1

SECTION 2: Combating Self-Criticism   33

SECTION 3: Learning to Accept and Appreciate Your Positive Qualities   75

Extra Charts and Worksheets   125

Introduction: How to Use this Workbook

This is a self-help course for dealing with low self-esteem. It has two aims:

1 To help you develop a better understanding of the problem

2 To teach you the practical skills you will need in order to change

How the course works

The *Overcoming Low Self-Esteem Self-Help Course* will help you understand how low self-esteem develops and what keeps it going, and then to make changes in your life so that you begin to feel more confident and more kindly and accepting towards yourself.

These workbooks are designed to help you work, either by yourself or with your healthcare practitioner, to overcome low self-esteem. With plenty of questionnaires, charts, worksheets and practical exercises, the three parts together make up a structured course.

Part One explained:

- What low self-esteem is

- How low self-esteem affects people

- How negative experiences affect people

- What keeps low self-esteem going

Part Two explains:

- How to recognize and deal with anxious predictions

- How to recognize and question self-critical thoughts

- How to identify your positive qualities

- How to gain a balanced view of yourself and start enjoying life

Part Three explains:

- What Rules for Living are

- How to change your Rules for Living

- How to recognize and change your central belief about yourself

- How to draft and fine-tune an Action Plan for the future

How long will the course take?

Each workbook will take at least two or three weeks to work through – but do not worry if you feel that you need to give each one extra time. Some things can be understood and changed quite quickly, but others take longer. You will know when you are ready to move on to the next workbook. Completing the entire course could take only two to three months, but this will depend on how quickly you wish to work. Take your time, and go at the pace that suits you best.

Getting the most from the course

Here are some tips to help you get the most from the workbooks:

- These workbooks are not priceless antiques – they are practical tools. So feel free not only to write on the worksheets and charts, but also to underline and highlight things, and to write comments and questions in the margins. By the time you have finished with a workbook, it should look well and truly used.

- You will also find lots of space in the main text. This is for you to write down your thoughts and ideas, and your responses to the questions.

- Keep an open mind and be willing to experiment with new ideas and skills. These workbooks will sometimes ask you to think about painful issues. However, if low self-esteem is distressing you and restricting your life, it really is worth making the effort to overcome it. The rewards will be substantial.

- Be prepared to invest time in doing the practical exercises – set aside 20 to 30 minutes each day if you can.

- Try to answer all the questions and do the exercises, even if you have to come back to some of them later. There may be times when you get stuck and can't think how to take things forward. If this happens, don't get angry with yourself or give up. Just put the workbook aside and come back to it later, when you are feeling more relaxed.

- You may find it helpful to work through the books with a friend. Two heads are often better than one. And you may be able to encourage each other to persist, even when one of you is finding it hard.

- Use the Thoughts and Reflections section at the back of the workbook to write down anything you read that has been particularly helpful to you.

- Re-read the workbook. You may get more out of it once you've had a chance to think about some of the ideas and put them into practice for a little while.

- Each workbook builds on what has already been covered. So what you learn when working with one will help you when you come to the next. It's quite possible simply to dip into different ones as you please, but you may get most out of the series if you follow them through systematically, step by step.

A note of caution

These workbooks will not help everyone who has low self-esteem. If you find that focusing on self-esteem is actually making you feel worse instead of better, or if your negative beliefs about yourself are so strong that you cannot even begin to use the ideas and practical skills described, you may be suffering from clinical depression. The recognized signs of clinical depression include:

- Constantly feeling sad, down, depressed or empty

- General lack of interest in what's going on around you

- A big increase or decrease in your appetite and weight

- A marked change in your sleep patterns

- Noticeable speeding up or slowing down in your movements and how you go about things

- Feeling of being tired and low in energy

- An intense sense of guilt or worthlessness

- Difficulty in concentrating and making decisions

- A desire to hurt yourself or a feeling that you might be better off dead

If you have had five or more of these symptoms (including low mood or loss of interest) for two weeks or more, you should seek professional help from a doctor, counsellor or psychotherapist. There is nothing shameful about seeking this sort of professional help – any more than there is anything shameful about taking your car to a garage if it is not working as it should, or going to see a lawyer if you have legal problems. It simply means taking your journey towards self-knowledge and self-acceptance with the help of a friendly guide, rather than striking out alone.

SECTION 1: Checking Out Anxious Predictions

This section will help you to understand:

- why we make predictions
- how anxious predictions keep low self-esteem going
- what anxious predictions are
- how to spot your own anxious predictions and the unnecessary precautions that you take to stop them from coming true
- how to find alternatives to your anxious predictions
- how to check out your anxious predictions in practice

Why do we make predictions?

We all make predictions (e.g. 'If I press this switch, the light will come on', 'If I have too much to drink, I will have a hangover') and then act on them. We use information from our experience to confirm our predictions or to change them. Acting on predictions is generally a useful way of behaving, as long as we are prepared to change our predictions in the light of new evidence.

Imagine that you're about to start a new job. Look at the following predictions and write 'A' next to the ones that sound anxious and 'R' next to the ones that sound realistic:

a 'My colleagues will probably be helpful.' _____

b 'I'm bound to get everything wrong.' _____

c 'I just know I won't be able to cope with the pressure.' _____

d 'I may find the work hard at first but I'll soon get the hang of it.' _____

e 'My colleagues will think I'm stupid and laugh at me behind my back.' _____

f 'If I make a mistake, they'll all think I'm an idiot for evermore.' _____

g 'I will be nervous on my first day but everyone gets nervous when they start a new job.' _____

h 'If I make a silly mistake, people will probably tease me a bit and then forget about it.' _____

Anxious predictions: **b, c, e, f**

Realistic predictions: **a, d, g, h**

> ### It's worth remembering...
>
> **If you have low self-esteem, you will probably treat your anxious predictions as facts rather than ideas, which may or may not turn out to be true. This makes it difficult to stand back and look at the evidence objectively.**

You are likely to make anxious predictions in situations where your **Bottom Line** (e.g. 'I'm stupid' or 'I'm unlovable') has been activated. Your Bottom Line is your central belief about yourself, and it is activated when you think there is a risk that one or more of your personal **Rules for Living** *might* be broken.

For example, if your Bottom Line is 'I'm stupid', your main Rule for Living might be 'It's better not to try than to fail.' The system would be activated by situations where there was a danger that you might fail. And if your Bottom Line is 'I'm un-lovable', your main Rule for Living might be 'Unless I do everything people expect of me, I will be rejected.' In this case, the system would be activated by situations where you feared you would not meet others' expectations.

If you are 100 per cent sure that your Rules *have* been broken, then you may bypass anxiety and head straight for confirmation of your Bottom Line, self-criticism and possible depression. If you think that your Rules *might* be broken – there is a risk, but you are not sure – you are more likely to feel anxious, doubtful and uncertain.

How anxious predictions keep low self-esteem going

Trigger situations

Situations in which Rules for Living might be broken

Activation of the Bottom Line

Depression

Anxious predictions

Anxiety

Self-critical thinking

Unhelpful behaviour

Confirmation of the Bottom Line

Doubt and uncertainty will lead you to wonder what is going to happen next (e.g. 'Will I be able to cope?' 'Will people like me?'). The answers to these questions – which are really predictions about what is likely to go wrong – spark anxiety, and lead you to take a whole range of precautions to prevent the worst from happening. Unfortunately, in the long run, these precautions rarely work. You just end up feeling that your Bottom Line has been confirmed or, at best, that you have had a narrow escape.

What are anxious predictions?

We make anxious predictions when we fear that we are about to break rules that are important to our sense of self-esteem.

Anxious Predictions

These predictions usually involve:

1 Overestimating the chances that something bad will happen

2 Overestimating how bad it will be if something bad does happen

3 Underestimating our ability to deal with the worst, if it happens

4 Underestimating outside factors, such as other people's support

Let's take Kate, from Part One, as an example to illustrate these different types of anxious predictions.

CASE STUDY: Kate

Kate was brought up by elderly, middle-class parents. At heart, both were good people who tried their best to give their only daughter a sound start in life. However, they both had difficulty in openly expressing affection. Their only means of showing how much they loved her was through caring for her practical needs. So, they were good at ensuring that Kate did her homework, in seeing that she ate a balanced diet, that she was well dressed and had a good range of books and toys.

They almost never touched her – there were no cuddles, no kisses, no pet names. At first, Kate was hardly aware of this. But once she began to see how openly loving other families were, she began to experience a sad emptiness at home. Kate concluded that their behaviour must reflect something about her. Her parents did their duty by her, but no more. It must mean she was fundamentally unlovable.

Her Bottom Line was that she was unlovable, and her Rules for Living were that if she failed to meet others' expectations she would be rejected, and that if she ever asked for her needs to be met she would be disappointed.

1 Overestimating the chances that something bad will happen

Kate worked in a hairdresser's. She and her colleagues took it in turns to go out and buy the lunchtime sandwiches. One day, when it was her turn, her boss forgot to pay her back for his sandwich. Kate felt completely unable to ask for what she was owed. She was convinced that, if she did so, her boss would despise her and think she was mean. This was despite the fact that she knew from months of working for him that he was a kind, thoughtful man who cared about his employees' welfare. She took no account of the evidence, which suggested that in fact he was likely to be embarrassed, apologize and immediately give her what she was entitled to.

In a situation where you think it will be hard to stick to your Rules for Living, you may get over-anxious that something will go wrong. Think of a time when you overestimated the chance that something bad would happen.

When and where did it happen?

_____

_____

_____

_____

What exactly did you think would happen (what was your prediction)?

_____

_____

_____

_____

2 Overestimating how bad it will be if something bad does happen

When Kate looked into the future, she could not see her boss being mildly inconvenienced by having to pay her back, and then quickly forgetting all about it. She assumed that asking for what he owed her would permanently change their relationship. He would never look at her in the same way again, and she would probably need to find another job – which would be difficult, because he would not want to give her a reference. Then she would have to go back to her parents' house and live on state benefits and would be completely stuck. Kate could clearly see all this happening, in her mind's eye.

At the heart of anxious predictions is the idea that the worst possible thing will happen and that, when it does, it won't be over quickly. Instead it will be a huge personal disaster. Think of a time when you overestimated how bad it would be if something bad did happen.

When and where did it happen?

_____

_____

_____

_____

What was your prediction about how bad things would be?

_____

_____

_____

_____

3 Underestimating your ability to deal with the worst, if it happens

Kate assumed that, no matter what she did, her boss would reject her. It did not occur to her that she could stand up to her boss, if he did indeed respond as she predicted, by reminding him that she was entitled to get her money back. Nor did she take account of her professional skill and experience, which in fact made it very likely that she would find other employment quite easily.

Anxiety may make you think that, if the worst does happen, there will be nothing you can do to prevent it or make it manageable. Think of a time when you underestimated your ability to deal with the worst.

When and where did it happen?

_____

_____

_____

_____

What was your prediction about how you would cope?

_____

_____

_____

_____

4 Underestimating outside factors such as other people's support

Kate completely overlooked the fact that she would get support from her colleagues, friends and family if her boss reacted so unreasonably.

Anxiety may lead you to underestimate things outside yourself that might improve the situation. Think of a time when you underestimated outside factors.

When and where did it happen?

_____

_____

_____

_____

What was your prediction about what outside factors might be there to help you?

_____

_____

_____

_____

How can you spot your anxious predictions and unnecessary precautions?

Anxious predictions give you a strong sense that you are at risk – of failure, of rejection, of losing control, of making a fool of yourself. So, like any sensible person facing a threat, you take precautions to stop the worst from happening. Unfortunately, these precautions, far from improving things, actually stop you from finding out for yourself whether your anxious predictions have any basis in reality.

To get a more realistic view of what is likely to happen in situations you fear, you need to become aware of your anxious predictions and the unnecessary precautions you take. The best way to do this is to keep a record for a few days, noticing what is running through your mind as soon as the anxiety starts, and spotting what you do to protect yourself. The chart filled in by Kate, on p. 8, illustrates how to go about it.

You will find other Predictions and Precautions Charts for you to fill in on pp. 9–15, and further guidelines to help you complete the charts on pp. 16–18.

Predictions and Precautions Chart: Kate

Date/Time	Situation What were you doing when you began to feel anxious?	Emotions and body sensations (e.g. anxious, panicky, tense, heart racing). Rate 0–100 for intensity.	Anxious predictions What exactly was going through your mind when you began to feel anxious (e.g. thoughts in words, images)? Rate 0–100% for degree of belief.	Precautions What did you do to stop your predictions coming true (e.g. avoid the situation, safety-seeking behaviours)?
6 February	Bought sandwich for Ian for lunch. He forgot to pay me back.	Anxious 85 Embarrassed 80 Heart racing 90 Sweaty 70 Hot 90	If I ask for the money, he will think I'm really mean 90% It will spoil our relationship forever 80% I will have to find another job 70% I won't be able to 70% I'll be stuck at home with no money 70%	Avoid him altogether If I *did* ask, I would: • be very apologetic • not look at him directly • keep my voice down • tell him it didn't really matter • get it over and done with as fast as possible and then run away

Predictions and Precautions Chart

Date/Time	Situation What were you doing when you began to feel anxious?	Emotions and body sensations (e.g. anxious, panicky, tense, heart racing). Rate 0–100 for intensity.	Anxious predictions What exactly was going through your mind when you began to feel anxious (e.g. thoughts in words, images)? Rate 0–100% for degree of belief.	Precautions What did you do to stop your predictions coming true (e.g. avoid the situation, safety-seeking behaviours)?

Predictions and Precautions Chart

Date/Time	Situation What were you doing when you began to feel anxious?	Emotions and body sensations (e.g. anxious, panicky, tense, heart racing). Rate 0–100 for intensity.	Anxious predictions What exactly was going through your mind when you began to feel anxious (e.g. thoughts in words, images)? Rate 0–100% for degree of belief.	Precautions What did you do to stop your predictions coming true (e.g. avoid the situation, safety-seeking behaviours)?

Predictions and Precautions Chart

Date/Time	Situation What were you doing when you began to feel anxious?	Emotions and body sensations (e.g. anxious, panicky, tense, heart racing). Rate 0–100 for intensity.	Anxious predictions What exactly was going through your mind when you began to feel anxious (e.g. thoughts in words, images)? Rate 0–100% for degree of belief.	Precautions What did you do to stop your predictions coming true (e.g. avoid the situation, safety-seeking behaviours)?

Predictions and Precautions Chart

Date/Time	Situation What were you doing when you began to feel anxious?	Emotions and body sensations (e.g. anxious, panicky, tense, heart racing). Rate 0–100 for intensity.	Anxious predictions What exactly was going through your mind when you began to feel anxious (e.g. thoughts in words, images)? Rate 0–100% for degree of belief.	Precautions What did you do to stop your predictions coming true (e.g. avoid the situation, safety-seeking behaviours)?

Predictions and Precautions Chart

Date/Time	Situation What were you doing when you began to feel anxious?	Emotions and body sensations (e.g. anxious, panicky, tense, heart racing). Rate 0–100 for intensity.	Anxious predictions What exactly was going through your mind when you began to feel anxious (e.g. thoughts in words, images)? Rate 0–100% for degree of belief.	Precautions What did you do to stop your predictions coming true (e.g. avoid the situation, safety-seeking behaviours)?

Predictions and Precautions Chart

Date/Time	Situation What were you doing when you began to feel anxious?	Emotions and body sensations (e.g. anxious, panicky, tense, heart racing). Rate 0–100 for intensity.	Anxious predictions What exactly was going through your mind when you began to feel anxious (e.g. thoughts in words, images)? Rate 0–100% for degree of belief.	Precautions What did you do to stop your predictions coming true (e.g. avoid the situation, safety-seeking behaviours)?

Predictions and Precautions Chart

Date/Time	Situation What were you doing when you began to feel anxious?	Emotions and body sensations (e.g. anxious, panicky, tense, heart racing). Rate 0–100 for intensity.	Anxious predictions What exactly was going through your mind when you began to feel anxious (e.g. thoughts in words, images)? Rate 0–100% for degree of belief.	Precautions What did you do to stop your predictions coming true (e.g. avoid the situation, safety-seeking behaviours)?

The information you gather will enable you to begin to question your predictions and check them out by doing the things you are afraid of without taking unnecessary precautions.

If at all possible, make your record when you actually experience the anxiety. It is often difficult to tune into anxious predictions when you are no longer feeling anxious. They may seem ridiculous or exaggerated when you are not in the situation, and so it will be difficult to accept how far you believed them and how anxious you felt at the time. Here are some guidelines to help you fill in each section.

Date/time

- When did you experience the anxiety?

- Can you see a pattern? For instance, do you tend to get anxious on weekdays at work, or at the weekends when you are expected to socialize?

The situation

- What was happening when you started to feel anxious? Where were you? Who were you with?

- Or was it that something uncomfortable came to mind – a memory perhaps, or a concern about something in the future?

Your feelings

- What emotions did you feel? Were you anxious, panicky, frightened, pressurized, worried, frustrated, irritable, impatient – or what?

- Rate each emotion between 0 and 100, according to how strong it was (100 would mean it was as strong as it could possibly be; 50 would mean it was moderately strong; 5 would mean there was just a hint of emotion, and so on).

Body sensations

- Did you feel your muscles tensing up – in your jaw, forehead, shoulders or hands?

- Did your heart feel as if it was speeding up, pounding heavily or missing a beat?

- Were you holding your breath, breathing faster or breathing unevenly?

- Was it hard to focus on what was going on? Did your mind go blank? Did you feel muddled or confused?

- Did you have problems with your digestion (e.g. churning stomach, 'butterflies', needing to go to the toilet repeatedly)?

- Did you have other physical symptoms (e.g. shakiness; sweating; feeling weak, dizzy or faint; numbness or tingling sensations; blurred or tunnel vision)?

- Make a note of your body sensations, and rate them between 0 and 100 according to how strong they were, just as you rated your emotions.

Your anxious predictions

- What was going through your mind just before you began to feel anxious? And as your anxiety built up?

- What did you think was going to go wrong, or was already going wrong? (Write down your predictions, word for word, just as they occur to you.)

- Did your predictions take the form of pictures in your mind's eye (snapshots or freeze frames, or a movie sequence with events following on from one another)?

- Were your predictions in the form of short exclamations, such as 'Oh my God!' or 'Here I go again'? (These exclamations are just other ways of making anxious predictions. Ask yourself what you thought was going to happen.)

- Or were your predictions in the form of questions, such as 'Will they like me?' (Look for the prediction hiding behind the question, e.g. 'They won't like me.')

- When you have written down your predictions, rate each one (verbal or visual) between 0 and 100 per cent, according to how strongly you believed it when you were at your most anxious. (100 per cent means you were fully convinced, with no shadow of doubt; 50 means you were in two minds; 5 means you thought there was a remote possibility; and so on.)

Your precautions

- What steps did you take to ensure that your predictions did not come true?

- Did you completely avoid the situation? Or did you enter the situation but take precautions to prevent yourself from breaking your Rules for Living?

- Write down what you did to protect yourself, in as much detail as possible.

Keep your record for a week, filling in one chart per day. By the end of the week, you should have a pretty good idea of the situations in which you feel anxious, the predictions that spark off your anxiety, and the precautions you take to prevent the worst from happening.

How can you find alternatives to your anxious predictions?

Anxious predictions make you feel bad and encourage you to take precautions that only keep the vicious circle of low self-esteem going. So, finding alternatives to them will help you to feel more confident.

The first step is to learn to stand back and question your predictions, rather than accepting them as fact. You can use the key questions listed on p. 23 to help you discover more helpful and realistic perspectives and tackle the negative (biased) thinking that contributes to anxiety. Each time you find an alternative to one of your anxious predictions, write it down on the chart on p. 20 and rate how far you believe it (from 0 to 100 per cent). You may well not believe your alternatives fully to begin with, but you should at least be prepared to accept that they might theoretically be true. Once you have a chance to test them out in practice, your degree of belief will increase. When you have found all the alternatives you can think of, move across to the final column on the chart to assess the outcome of what you have done. Now that you have found alternatives to your predictions, how do you feel? And how far do you now believe your original predictions (0–100 per cent)? You may not have stopped believing in them completely. Once again, this is where checking them out in practice will be helpful.

The **Questioning Anxious Predictions Chart** filled in by Kate (p. 19) will give you a sense of how to go about questioning your predictions and finding more realistic and helpful alternatives to them.

You will find blank **Questioning Anxious Predictions Charts** for you to fill in on pp. 20–22. Aim to complete the sheets for at least three days, using one chart per day. This will give you a chance to use these new skills in a range of situations. Feel free to continue beyond three days if you feel it would be helpful. You will find further guidelines to help you complete the charts on pp. 23–25.

Questioning Anxious Predictions Chart: Kate

Date/Time	Situation	Emotions and body sensations Rate 0–100% for intensity.	Anxious predictions Rate belief 0–100%.	Alternative perspectives Use the key questions to find other views of the situation. Rate belief 0–100%.	Outcome 1. What did you do instead of taking your usual precautions? 2. What were the results?
20 Feb.	Ask Ian for money he owes me.	Anxious 95% Embarrassed 95% Heart pounding 95% Feeling hot and red 100%	He will shout at me 90%	There's no evidence he'll react like that. What I know of him shows he's not that kind of person 100%	1. Ask him. Don't apologize or say it doesn't matter. Be polite and pleasant, but firm. Take your time.
			He'll think I'm really mean 90%	He might be a bit annoyed, but it would pass and he'd be thinking of something else two minutes later 95%	2. He gave it to me right away! He said he was sorry, he'd just forgotten. No sign afterwards that he thought anything of it.
			It will spoil our relationship forever 80%	Even if he did react like that, everyone would support me. I would if it was someone else. I would think they were entitled to what they were owed 100%	I learned that if I take the risk, I can get what I want, even if it does make me nervous.
			I will have to find another job 80%	Maybe I'm entitled too 30%	
			I won't be able to 70%	Even if I did lose my job, I'm a good enough hairdresser to find another 60%	
			I'll be stuck at home with no money 70%	I could be making a mountain out of a molehill here 50%	

Questioning Anxious Predictions Chart

Date/Time	Situation	Emotions and body sensations Rate 0–100% for intensity.	Anxious predictions Rate belief 0–100%.	Alternative perspectives Use the key questions to find other views of the situation. Rate belief 0–100%.	Outcome 1. How do you now feel (emotions, body sensations)? 2. How far do you now believe your original predictions (0–100%)?

Questioning Anxious Predictions Chart

Date/Time	Situation	Emotions and body sensations Rate 0–100% for intensity.	Anxious predictions Rate belief 0–100%.	Alternative perspectives Use the key questions to find other views of the situation. Rate belief 0–100%.	Outcome 1. How do you now feel (emotions, body sensations)? 2. How far do you now believe your original predictions (0–100%)?

Questioning Anxious Predictions Chart

Date/Time	Situation	Emotions and body sensations Rate 0–100% for intensity.	Anxious predictions Rate belief 0–100%.	Alternative perspectives Use the key questions to find other views of the situation. Rate belief 0–100%.	Outcome 1. How do you now feel (emotions, body sensations)? 2. How far do you now believe your original predictions (0–100%)?

> ## Key Questions
>
> ### To Help You Find Alternatives to Anxious Predictions
>
> **1** What is the evidence to support what you are predicting?
>
> **2** What is the evidence against what you are predicting?
>
> **3** What alternative views are there? What evidence is there to support them?
>
> **4** What is the worst that can happen?
>
> **5** What is the best that can happen?
>
> **6** Realistically, what is most likely to happen?
>
> **7** If the worst happens, what could be done about it?

Here are some guidelines to help you answer the key questions and fill in your chart.

1 What is the evidence to support what you are predicting?

- What makes you expect the worst?

- Are there experiences in the past (either recently or earlier in your life) that have led you to expect disaster now?

- Is your main evidence simply your own feelings?

- Or is it just a habit? Do you always expect things to go wrong in this sort of situation? Are you jumping to conclusions, instead of keeping an open mind?

2 What is the evidence against what you are predicting?

- What are the facts of the current situation? Do they support what you think, or do they contradict it?

- In particular, can you find any evidence that does *not* fit your predictions?

- Is there anything you have been ignoring that would suggest that your fears might be exaggerated?

- Are there any resources you could draw on, either in yourself or around you, that you have not been taking into account?

- Have you had any previous experience that suggests things may not go as badly as you fear?

3 What alternative views are there? What evidence is there to support them?

- How would you view this challenging situation if, for example, you were feeling less anxious and more confident?

- What might another person make of it?

- What would you say to a friend who came to you with the same anxiety – would your predictions be different for them?

- Are you exaggerating the importance of the event?

- How will you see this event after a week? A month? A year? Ten years?

- Will anyone even remember what happened? Will you? If so, will you still feel the same about it?

Write down the alternative perspectives you have found, and then make sure you review the evidence for and against them, just as you reviewed the evidence for and against your original predictions. An alternative that does not fit the facts will not be helpful to you, so make sure that your alternatives are realistic.

4 What is the worst that can happen?

This question is particularly useful in dealing with anxious predictions, because it helps to highlight exaggerations. Look for whatever information you need to obtain a more realistic estimate of the true likelihood of what you fear occurring. Even if it is not impossible, it may be much less likely to happen than you predict.

- Can you visualize the very worst that can happen in vivid detail?

- Does it seem exaggerated or unrealistic?

- Is it likely or even possible?

5 What is the best that can happen?

- Imagine the best possible outcome, to counter-balance your worst. Make it just as positive as your worst is negative.

- Are you less inclined to believe in the best than you were to believe in the worst?

- Why? Could your thinking be biased in some way?

6 Realistically, what is most likely to happen?

- Look at the best and worst possibilities, and see if you can work out, *realistically*, what is actually most likely to happen. (The answer will probably lie somewhere between the best and the worst.)

7 If the worst happens, what could be done about it?

- Just supposing the worst did happen, what personal assets and skills do you have that would help you to deal with it?

- What past experience do you have of successfully dealing with other, similar threats?

- What help, advice and support are available to you from other people?

- What information could you get that would help you to gain a full picture of what is going on and deal more effectively with the situation? Who could you ask? What other sources of information are open to you (e.g. books, the media, the Internet)?

- What can you do to change the situation itself? If the situation that makes you anxious is genuinely unsatisfactory in some way, what changes do you need to make?

Perhaps someone's unreasonable expectations of you need to change, or you need to begin doing more for yourself, or to organize extra help and support. You may well find that such changes are blocked by further negative predictions (e.g. 'But they'll be angry with me') or by self-critical thoughts (e.g. 'But I should be able to cope alone'). If so, make a note of these thoughts and search for alternatives to them. They, too, can be questioned and tested out.

How can you check out your anxious predictions in practice?

Questioning your thoughts may not be enough in itself to convince you that things are better than they seem. You need to act differently, too, to learn how things really are through direct experience. Experimenting with new ways of doing things (for example, being more assertive or accepting challenges you would previously have avoided) enables you to break old habits of thinking and strengthen new ones. These experiments give you an opportunity to find out for yourself whether the alternatives you have found are in line with the facts, and therefore helpful to you, or whether you need to think again. But this will happen only if you take the risk of entering situations you have been avoiding, and drop the precautions you have been taking to keep yourself safe.

You can set up these experiments quite deliberately (e.g. planning and carrying out one experiment each day), and you can also use situations that arise without you planning them (e.g. an unexpected phone call or an invitation) to practise acting differently and observing the outcome. Record the results for at least three days, so that you have a chance to experiment in a range of situations. Feel free to continue beyond three days if you feel it would be helpful. You can use the **Using Experiments to Check Out Anxious Predictions Chart** on pp. 27–29 to record what you do.

You will also find a further blank chart at the back of the book and guidelines to help you fill the charts in on pp. 30–32.

Using Experiments to Check Out Anxious Predictions Chart

Date/Time	Situation	Anxious predictions Rate belief 0–100%.	Experiment What will I do instead of taking precautions?	Results 1. What have you learned? 2. Were your predictions correct? If not, what perspective would make better sense?

Using Experiments to Check Out Anxious Predictions Chart

Date/Time	Situation	Anxious predictions Rate belief 0–100%.	Experiment What will I do instead of taking precautions?	Results 1. What have you learned? 2. Were your predictions correct? If not, what perspective would make better sense?

Using Experiments to Check Out Anxious Predictions Chart

Date/Time	Situation	Anxious predictions Rate belief 0–100%.	Experiment What will I do instead of taking precautions?	Results 1. What have you learned? 2. Were your predictions correct? If not, what perspective would make better sense?

Here are some guidelines to help you fill in your chart.

1 State your prediction clearly

It is particularly important to specify your anxious predictions clearly when you come to check them out in action – if your predictions are vague or unclear, you will find it hard to judge whether they are really correct or not. So, as before, write down exactly what you expect to happen, including how you think you will react, and rate each prediction according to how strongly you believe it (from 0 to 100 per cent). For example, if you are predicting that you will feel bad, rate in advance how bad you think you will feel (from 0 to 100 per cent), and in what way. Many people find that, to their surprise, they do indeed feel anxious (for example), but not as much as they expected, especially once they get over the initial hurdle of entering the feared situation. Your rating will give you a chance to find out if this is true for you.

Your predictions may also involve other people's reactions. Perhaps you think that if you behave in a given way, people will lose interest in you, or disapprove of you. If so, how would you know? How would they show that they were indeed losing interest or disapproving? Include comments, gestures, and small signs like changes in facial expression, and shifts in direction of gaze. This will tell you exactly what to look for when you go into the situation.

2 What will you do, instead of taking precautions to ensure that your predictions do not come true?

Use the work you have already done on identifying anxious predictions and precautions to think of all the things you might be tempted to do to protect yourself (no matter how small), and work out in advance what you will do instead. For example:

● If your normal pattern when you talk to someone is to avoid eye contact and say as little as possible about yourself, in case people discover how boring you are, your new pattern might be to look at people, and talk as much about yourself as they do about themselves.

● If your normal pattern at work is to have an answer to every question and never admit to ignorance, in case people think you are not up to the job, you could practise saying 'I don't know' or 'I have no opinion on that'.

● If your normal pattern is to hide your feelings, because to show them at all could lead you to lose control, you might experiment with being a little more open with someone you trust, about something that has upset you, or with showing affection more openly than you normally would.

3 What were the results of your experiment?

Always review the results of your experiment afterwards. Ask yourself:

- What did you learn?

- What impact did acting differently have on how you felt?

- How closely did what happened match your original predictions? And how far did it match the alternatives you found?

- What have you discovered about your negative view of yourself – your Bottom Line? Does what happened actually confirm your Bottom Line? Or does the result of the experiment suggest that you could afford to think more kindly of yourself?

On the one hand, your experience may show that your anxious predictions were *not* correct, and that the alternatives you found were indeed more realistic and helpful.

On the other hand, your experience may show your anxious predictions to be absolutely correct. If so, do not despair. Just ask yourself some more questions:

- How did this come about?

- Was it in fact anything to do with you, or some other element of the situation?

- What other explanations might there be for what went wrong, besides you?

- If you did contribute in some way to what happened, is there any way you could handle the situation differently in future, so as to bring about a different result? For example, are you sure you dropped *all* your precautions?

- If some precautions were still in place, what do you think might have happened if you had dropped them (anxious predictions)? How could you check this out? Exactly what changes do you still need to make to your behaviour?

- How will you ensure that you drop your precautions completely, next time?

When you have carefully thought through what happened, work out what experiments you need to carry out next. Ask yourself:

- How could you apply what you have learned in other situations?

- What further action do you need to take?

- Should you repeat the same experiment to build your confidence in the results?

- Or should you try similar changes in a new and perhaps more challenging situation?

- What does what happened tell you about yourself, other people and how the world works?

- Given what has happened, what predictions would make better sense next time you tackle this type of situation?

- Based on what happened in this particular situation, what general strategies could you adopt to help you deal even more effectively with similar situations in future?

Whatever the outcome of your experiment, congratulate yourself for what you have done. Giving yourself credit for facing challenges is part of learning to accept and value yourself.

Summary

1   In situations where your Rules for Living *might* be broken, your Bottom Line is activated and triggers predictions about what could go wrong.

2   Such predictions usually involve: overestimating the chances that something will go wrong; overestimating how bad it would be if it did go wrong; and underestimating your personal resources and factors outside yourself which could help to make the situation more manageable.

3   To prevent your predictions from coming true, you take unnecessary precautions which make it impossible to discover if the predictions are correct or not.

4   In order to tackle anxious predictions, you need to learn to spot them as they occur, and observe their impact on your emotions and body state, and the unnecessary precautions they lead you to take.

5   The next step is to question your predictions, examining the evidence that supports and contradicts them, and searching for alternative, more realistic perspectives.

6   The final step is to gain direct evidence of how accurate your predictions and your new alternatives are. You can do this by setting up experiments – facing situations that you normally avoid, and dropping your unnecessary precautions.

SECTION 2: Combating Self-Criticism

This section will help you to understand:

- what impact self-criticism has on you
- why self-criticism does more harm than good
- how you can become more aware of your self-critical thoughts
- how to question self-critical thoughts
- how to use key questions to help you find alternatives to self-critical thoughts

What impact does self-criticism have on you?

Tick the responses that most closely match the way you behave when something goes wrong or you make a mistake. Do you usually:

- **a** call yourself names?
- **b** tell yourself you should do better?
- **c** see a single mistake as evidence that you are a stupid/incompetent/inadequate person?
- **d** ignore the things you got right and concentrate on what you got wrong?
- **e** blame yourself entirely, ignoring any outside factors that may have caused you to make the mistake?

If you have ticked more than one response, you are behaving in a way that is typical of someone with low self-esteem. People with low self-esteem notice some difficulty, or something wrong about themselves, and on that basis make judgements about themselves as whole people ('stupid', 'incompetent', 'unattractive', 'rotten mother', etc.). These judgements completely ignore the other side of the picture. The end result is a biased point of view, rather than a balanced perspective. The bias expresses itself in self-critical thoughts, which result in painful feelings (sadness, disappointment, anger, guilt), and keep low self-esteem going.

You can get some sense of the emotional impact of self-critical thoughts by carrying out the following experiment. Read the list of words printed over the page, carefully, allowing each one to sink in.

Imagine they apply to you, and notice their impact on your mood. Give each one a score, from 0 (no impact on your mood), through -5 (makes you feel quite bad), to -10 (makes you feel really awful):

Useless ____	Unattractive ____	Incompetent ____
Weak ____	Unlikeable ____	Ugly ____
Pathetic ____	Unwanted ____	Stupid ____
Worthless ____	Inferior ____	Inadequate ____

Some of the words on the list may be familiar to you, from your own self-critical thoughts. If so, highlight or underline them. What other words do you use to describe yourself when you are being self-critical? Make a note of them. These are words you will need to watch out for.

This section will move you towards a more balanced and accepting view of yourself by helping you to learn to notice when you are being self-critical, and to observe carefully the impact self-criticism has on your feelings and how you behave in day-to-day situations.

This is the part of the vicious circle we shall be working on:

How self-criticism keeps low self-esteem going

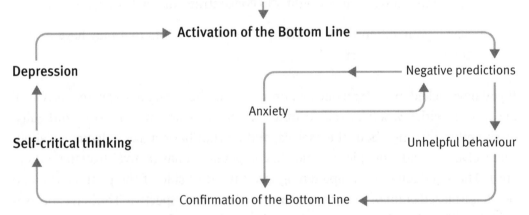

Trigger situations

Situations in which Rules for Living might be broken or have been broken

Activation of the Bottom Line

Depression

Negative predictions

Anxiety

Self-critical thinking

Unhelpful behaviour

Confirmation of the Bottom Line

In this section, you will learn how to question self-critical thoughts and to search for kinder alternatives, just as you learned to question your anxious predictions. The next section teaches you how to become more aware of positive aspects of yourself, and how to give more weight to your strengths, assets, qualities and talents.

Why does self-criticism do more harm than good?

In many cultures, people believe that thinking well of themselves is equivalent to boasting and big-headedness. This is why children are often taught to behave better and work harder by having their faults emphasized, rather than by having their successes praised. Parents and teachers may spend their time pointing out what children have done wrong, instead of helping them to build on what they have done right.

So self-critical thinking is often learned early in life. It becomes a habit – something you do automatically without thinking about it. You may even see it as helpful and constructive. But in fact self-criticism has some serious disadvantages.

> *Key Disadvantages of Self-Criticism*
>
> **Self-criticism:**
>
> - **paralyses you and makes you feel bad**
> - **is unfair**
> - **blocks learning**
> - **ignores the realities**
> - **kicks you when you are down**

Self-criticism paralyses you and makes you feel bad

Imagine a person you know who is quite self-confident. Imagine following them around, pointing out every little mistake they make, calling them names, telling them what they have done is all very well but could have been done better/faster/more effectively. As the days and weeks went by, what effect would you expect this constant drip, drip, drip of criticism to have?

How would they feel?

_____

_____

_____

_____

_____

How would it affect their confidence?

_____

_____

_____

_____

_____

_____

How would it influence their ability to make decisions?

_____

_____

_____

_____

_____

Would it make life easier for them, or more difficult?

_____

_____

_____

_____

_____

Would you even consider doing this to a friend of yours?

_____

_____

_____

_____

_____

If not, why not?

_____

_____

_____

_____

_____

_____

_____

_____

If you have the habit of self-critical thinking, then this is probably what you are doing to yourself, perhaps without even being particularly aware of it. Self-critical thoughts are like a parrot on your shoulder, constantly squawking disapproval in your ear. Consider how this may be discouraging and demoralizing you, and paralysing your efforts to change and grow.

Self-criticism is unfair

Being self-critical means that you react to mistakes, failures or errors of judgement – even very small ones – as if they told the whole story about you. When you notice a single fault or weakness, you use it as a reason to tell yourself you are bad, pathetic or stupid *as a person*.

Do you think this is fair? _____

Would you think it was fair to treat another person in the same way?

_____

When you condemn yourself as a person on the basis of an error or something you regret, you are drawing a general conclusion about yourself on the basis of biased evidence, taking only negative aspects of yourself into account. Be realistic: give yourself credit for your assets and strengths as well as acknowledging that, like the rest of the human race, you have weaknesses and flaws.

Self-criticism blocks learning

Self-criticism undermines your confidence and makes you feel discouraged, demoralized and bad about yourself.

How much will this help you to overcome your problems, and alter those aspects of yourself that you genuinely want to change?

_____

_____

_____

_____

Does self-criticism give you any clues as to how to do better next time?

_____

_____

_____

_____

Do you think people learn more when their successes are praised or when they are punished for their failures?

_____

_____

_____

_____

If you pay attention only to what you do wrong, you lose the opportunity to learn from and repeat what you do right. Similarly, if you write yourself off every time you make an error, you lose the opportunity to learn from your mistakes and to work constructively on aspects of yourself that you wish to change.

Self-criticism ignores the realities

When things go wrong, in addition to criticizing yourself for what you did, you probably tell yourself you *should* have acted differently. With hindsight, it is often easy to see how you could have handled things better. But how did things appear to you *at the time*?

What was happening?

_____

_____

_____

_____

_____

How were you feeling?

_____

_____

_____

_____

_____

Were you thinking clearly?

_____

_____

_____

_____

_____

_____

Did you have all the information you needed to deal with the situation in the best possible way?

_____

_____

_____

_____

_____

Taking all these circumstances into account, it's probably completely understandable that you acted as you did, even if it turned out not to be in your best interests. This does not mean letting yourself off the hook if you genuinely did do something you regret. But you can learn from experiences by looking back at them. Then, if a similar situation arises again, you will have a different perspective on how to deal with it. Punishing yourself by brooding on past mistakes will only make you feel bad. It will not help you to think more clearly and do better next time.

Self-criticism kicks you when you are down

People with low self-esteem sometimes criticize themselves for the problems they are experiencing (e.g. anxiety, depression, lack of assertiveness). They may even criticize themselves for not being more self-confident. This lack of compassion ignores the fact that we all have difficulties of one kind or another, and that they are normally an understandable result of our experiences in life. It just makes you feel even more undermined and demoralized.

If other people had experienced the difficulties you have encountered in your life, what sort of problems might they have?

_____

_____

_____

_____

_____

Is it possible that your difficulties (including how you think about yourself) are a natural reaction to stressful events?

_____

_____

_____

_____

_____

If you had a friend with similar difficulties, developed under the same circumstances, what advice would you give to him or her?

_____

_____

_____

_____

_____

In all probability, anyone who had experienced what you have experienced would see themselves as you do. With the help of these workbooks, and other resources if necessary, you will be able to find ways to manage self-criticism and its consequences more successfully. What is certain is that criticizing yourself for having difficulties will not help you to resolve them.

The skills involved in dealing with self-critical thoughts are very similar to those you used when you were learning how to test anxious predictions. They are:

- Becoming more aware of your self-critical thoughts by recording them on charts

- Questioning your self-critical thoughts

- Experimenting with viewing yourself more compassionately

How can you become more aware of your self-critical thoughts?

The first step is to notice when you put yourself down, and to observe what impact it has on how you feel and behave. Your emotions can be a signal that self-critical thinking is going on. For this reason, it is helpful to learn to recognize them when they occur.

Think of a time when you did something you regretted:

When and where did the incident happen?

_____

_____

_____

_____

_____

Who was there?

_____

_____

_____

_____

_____

What happened?

_____

_____

_____

_____

_____

What did you say to yourself afterwards?

_____

_____

_____

_____

Tick the feelings you experienced:

☐ Guilty   ☐ Ashamed

☐ Sad   ☐ Embarrassed

☐ Disappointed in yourself ☐ Angry with yourself

☐ Frustrated   ☐ Depressed

☐ Hopeless   ☐ Despairing

Filling in a **Spotting Self-Critical Thoughts Chart** (see pp. 47–54) will help you to notice what is running through your mind when you feel bad about yourself, and to understand more clearly how these thoughts keep the vicious circle of low self-esteem going. You may well find that the same thoughts (or very similar ones) occur again and again. There is another blank chart at the back of the book, which you can photocopy if you wish.

Let's take Jim, from Part One of this course, as an example of how to keep this kind of record. You may remember that Jim accidentally knocked down and killed a woman who stepped off the pavement in front of him. At one point, after several months of being troubled by what happened, Jim had a few days of feeling considerably better. The accident seemed to be playing on his mind rather less, and he had been feeling more relaxed, more on top of things and like his normal self.

Then, one day, his daughter was very late home from school. Jim was terrified. He was certain something terrible had happened to her. In fact, he had forgotten that she was going to a friend's house. When she came in, he went ballistic. Afterwards, he felt thoroughly ashamed of himself. What a way to behave! 'This proves it,' he thought. 'I am really losing it. I'm a total mess.' He felt more and more upset. 'Pull yourself together,' he said to himself. 'This is pathetic. Get a grip.' The episode confirmed his worst suspicions about himself: he _was_ a nervous wreck, there was no doubt about it. And there seemed little chance of change. Jim was just about ready to give up.

You will find Jim's completed chart over the page.

Spotting Self-Critical Thoughts Chart: Jim

Date/Time	Situation What were you doing when you began to feel bad about yourself?	Emotions and body sensations (e.g. sad, angry, guilty). Rate each 0–100 for intensity.	Self-critical thoughts What exactly was going through your mind when you began to feel bad about yourself (e.g. thoughts in words, images, meanings)? Rate each 0–100% for degree of belief.	Self-defeating behaviour What did you do as a consequence of your self-critical thoughts?
5 March	Got in a rage with Kelly when she came home late. Had completely forgotten she was going to Jan's house.	Guilty 80 Fed up with myself 100 Hopeless 95	This proves it – I'm really losing it 100% I'm a total mess 95% I should pull myself together 100% This is pathetic 100% What's the matter with me? I just don't think I'll ever get back to how I was 95%	Stomped out of the house and went to the pub. Came back late and shut myself in the basement alone to watch TV. Didn't talk to anyone.

The Spotting Self-Critical Thoughts Chart

The best way to tune into self-critical thoughts is to make a note of them as soon as they occur. This is the first step to questioning them and searching for more helpful and realistic alternatives, just as you did with anxious predictions. Over the course of a few days, completing the chart will help you to recognize the changes in your feelings that signal the presence of self-critical thoughts.

Keep your record for about a week, filling in one chart every day. By then, you should have a pretty good idea of the kind of situations that spark self-critical thinking, and its impact on your emotions and what you do. Here are some guidelines to help you fill in the charts:

Date and time

- When did you feel bad about yourself?

You can use this information to pick up patterns over time, as you did with your anxious predictions.

The situation

- What was happening at the moment you began to feel bad about yourself?
- Where were you?
- Who were you with?
- What were you doing?

Briefly describe what was going on (e.g. 'asked a girl for a dance – she turned me down' or 'boss asked me to rewrite a report'). Perhaps you weren't doing anything in particular (e.g. washing up or watching television), and your self-critical thinking was triggered by something in your own mind. In this case, write down the general topic you were focusing on (e.g. 'thinking about my ex-husband taking the children for the weekend' or 'remembering being bullied at school'). Your exact thoughts, word for word, belong in the 'Self-critical thoughts' column.

Emotions and body sensations

- Did you feel one main emotion (e.g. sadness)?
- Or did you experience a mixture of emotions (e.g. not only sadness, but also guilt and anger)?

- Did you also experience changes in your body state (e.g. a sinking feeling or a churning stomach)?

Rate each emotion and body sensation between 0 and 100, according to how strong it was. (A rating of 5 would mean just a very faint emotional reaction or physical change; a rating of 50 would mean a moderate level of distress; and a rating of 100 would mean the emotion or sensation was as strong as it could possibly be.)

Self-critical thoughts

- What was running through your mind when you began to feel bad about yourself?

- Did you hear a voice in your mind, calling you names or telling you that you should have done better?

- Or did your thoughts take the form of images in your mind's eye?

- If you cannot identify any particular thoughts or images, ask: what does the situation tell you about yourself? What does it imply about what others think of you? What does it say about your future?

Rate each self-critical thought, image or meaning between 0 per cent and 100 per cent, according to how far you believed it when it occurred. (A rating of 100 per cent would mean you believed it completely, with no shadow of doubt; 50 per cent would mean you were in two minds; 5 per cent would mean you only believed it slightly.)

Self-defeating behaviour

What impact did your self-critical thoughts have on your behaviour? For example:

- Did you apologize for yourself?

- Did you withdraw into your shell?

- Did you avoid asking for something you needed?

- Did you allow yourself to be treated like a doormat or ignored?

- Did you avoid an opportunity that you might otherwise have taken?

On pp. 55–6 you will find the most frequently asked questions about the **Spotting Self-Critical Thoughts Chart**.

Spotting Self-Critical Thoughts Chart

Date/Time	Situation What were you doing when you began to feel bad about yourself?	Emotions and body sensations (e.g. sad, angry, guilty). Rate each 0–100 for intensity.	Self-critical thoughts What exactly was going through your mind when you began to feel bad about yourself (e.g. thoughts in words, images, meanings)? Rate each 0–100% for degree of belief.	Self-defeating behaviour What did you do as a consequence of your self-critical thoughts?

Spotting Self-Critical Thoughts Chart

Date/Time	Situation What were you doing when you began to feel bad about yourself?	Emotions and body sensations (e.g. sad, angry, guilty). Rate each 0–100 for intensity.	Self-critical thoughts What exactly was going through your mind when you began to feel bad about yourself (e.g. thoughts in words, images, meanings)? Rate each 0–100% for degree of belief.	Self-defeating behaviour What did you do as a consequence of your self-critical thoughts?

Spotting Self-Critical Thoughts Chart

| Date/Time | Situation
What were you doing when you began to feel bad about yourself? | Emotions and body sensations
(e.g. sad, angry, guilty). Rate each 0–100 for intensity. | Self-critical thoughts
What exactly was going through your mind when you began to feel bad about yourself (e.g. thoughts in words, images, meanings)? Rate each 0–100% for degree of belief. | Self-defeating behaviour
What did you do as a consequence of your self-critical thoughts? |
|---|---|---|---|---|
| | | | | |

Spotting Self-Critical Thoughts Chart

Date/Time	Situation What were you doing when you began to feel bad about yourself?	Emotions and body sensations (e.g. sad, angry, guilty). Rate each 0–100 for intensity.	Self-critical thoughts What exactly was going through your mind when you began to feel bad about yourself (e.g. thoughts in words, images, meanings)? Rate each 0–100% for degree of belief.	Self-defeating behaviour What did you do as a consequence of your self-critical thoughts?

Spotting Self-Critical Thoughts Chart

| Date/Time | Situation
What were you doing when you began to feel bad about yourself? | Emotions and body sensations
(e.g. sad, angry, guilty). Rate each 0–100 for intensity. | Self-critical thoughts
What exactly was going through your mind when you began to feel bad about yourself (e.g. thoughts in words, images, meanings)? Rate each 0–100% for degree of belief. | Self-defeating behaviour
What did you do as a consequence of your self-critical thoughts? |
|---|---|---|---|---|
| | | | | |

Spotting Self-Critical Thoughts Chart

Date/Time	Situation What were you doing when you began to feel bad about yourself?	Emotions and body sensations (e.g. sad, angry, guilty). Rate each 0–100 for intensity.	Self-critical thoughts What exactly was going through your mind when you began to feel bad about yourself (e.g. thoughts in words, images, meanings)? Rate each 0–100% for degree of belief.	Self-defeating behaviour What did you do as a consequence of your self-critical thoughts?

Spotting Self-Critical Thoughts Chart

Date/Time	Situation What were you doing when you began to feel bad about yourself?	Emotions and body sensations (e.g. sad, angry, guilty). Rate each 0–100 for intensity.	Self-critical thoughts What exactly was going through your mind when you began to feel bad about yourself (e.g. thoughts in words, images, meanings)? Rate each 0–100% for degree of belief.	Self-defeating behaviour What did you do as a consequence of your self-critical thoughts?

Spotting Self-Critical Thoughts Chart

Date/Time	Situation What were you doing when you began to feel bad about yourself?	Emotions and body sensations (e.g. sad, angry, guilty). Rate each 0–100 for intensity.	Self-critical thoughts What exactly was going through your mind when you began to feel bad about yourself (e.g. thoughts in words, images, meanings)? Rate each 0–100% for degree of belief.	Self-defeating behaviour What did you do as a consequence of your self-critical thoughts?

Frequently asked questions about the Spotting the Self-Critical Thoughts Chart

Here are some of the questions people often ask about filling in the **Spotting Self-Critical Thoughts Chart**.

Why is it important to fill it in?

Having a record in black and white means you have something concrete to reflect on, and there is less chance of you forgetting incidents. You can notice repeating patterns, consider how your thoughts affect your behaviour in different situations and become aware of the exact words you use to yourself when you are being self-critical.

Writing down your thoughts also takes them out of your head (so to speak), and allows you to stand back from them, take a good look at them and gain a different perspective. This will help you to move towards the point where you can begin to say, 'Uh oh, there's another one of those,' and to see them as something you do, rather than a true reflection of yourself.

How many thoughts do I need to record?

You could start by noting one or two self-critical thoughts each day. When observing their impact has become fairly automatic, you will be ready to move on to finding alternatives to your self-critical thoughts. This could take up to a week – but you may find you get the hang of it more quickly than that.

When should I make the record?

As with anxious predictions, the ideal is to write down your self-critical thoughts as soon as they occur. This will mean keeping your record sheets with you. The reason for this is that, although self-critical thoughts can have a very powerful effect when they actually occur, it may be hard afterwards to remember exactly what ran through your mind.

Of course, the ideal is not always possible. If you cannot write down what happened at the time, make sure that at least you make a mental note of what upset you, or jot down a reminder on any handy piece of paper. Then set aside time later to make a proper, detailed written record. Run through an 'action replay' in your mind – remember as vividly as you can where you were and what you were doing, the moment when you started to feel bad about yourself, what was running through your mind at that moment, and what you did in response to your thoughts.

Won't focusing on my self-critical thoughts just upset me?

It is natural to want to avoid focusing on upsetting ideas. You may feel understandably reluctant to commit these damning judgements of yourself to paper. But if you want to combat your self-critical thoughts effectively, you first need to look them in the face. So beware of excuses ('I'll do it later', 'It doesn't do to dwell on things'). Making excuses will deprive you of the chance to develop a more kindly perspective on yourself. And ignoring the thoughts will not make them go away.

How can you question your self-critical thoughts?

Developing awareness of your self-critical thoughts is the first step towards questioning them. The aim is to stop taking your self-critical thoughts as if they were statements of the truth about yourself, and to begin to find alternative perspectives that will provide you with a more balanced view.

You can use the **Combating Self-Critical Thoughts Chart** to help you do this. You will find one of Jim's completed charts on p. 57 as an illustration.

You will see that the first four columns of this sheet are identical to **Spotting Self-Critical Thoughts** (date/time; situation; emotions/body sensations; self-critical thoughts). However, the new chart does not stop there. Jim has also been asked to record 'alternative perspectives' and 'outcome' (just as you did when you questioned your anxious predictions).

On pp. 66–8 there are some more guidelines and frequently asked questions to help you fill in these extra columns on your own **Combating Self-Critical Thoughts Charts** on pp. 58–64. There is another blank chart at the back of the workbook, which you can photocopy if you wish.

Alternative perspectives

On page 65 there is a Key Questions box. You can use the these Key Questions to help you think of alternative perspectives. Rate each alternative according to how far you believe it, just as you rated the original self-critical thoughts (100 per cent if you believe it completely, 0 per cent if you do not believe it at all, and so on). You do not have to believe all your answers 100 per cent. They should, however, be sufficiently convincing to make at least some difference to how you feel. Each question is discussed in more detail later, on pp. 68–72.

Combating Self-Critical Thoughts Chart: Jim

Date/Time	Situation	Emotions and body sensations Rate each 0–100 for intensity.	Self-critical thoughts Rate each 0–100% for degree of belief.	Alternative perspectives Use the key questions to find other perspectives on yourself. Rate each 0–100% for degree of belief.	Outcome 1. Now that you have found alternatives to your self-critical thoughts, how do you feel (0–100)? 2. How far do you now believe the self-critical thoughts (0–100%)? 3. What can you do (action plan, experiments)?
8 March	Had a row with Kelly again. She wanted to go out on a friend's motorbike.	Guilty 80 Angry with myself 100 Hopeless 90	Here I go again, losing my temper over nothing. I am a wreck 100% I've got to get a grip on myself or I'll ruin everything 100% There's no end to this 90%	It's true that I was angrier than the situation warranted. But it's because I get frightened for her. Bikes are quite dangerous and I'm afraid of losing her. So it wasn't really about nothing. 100% I do need to do something about all this, it's true. I have changed a lot. But then, I went through something really bad, so maybe it's not surprising I'm not my usual self. 90% Rows are not good for any of us. But in fact we usually get over it. She's a good girl, even if a bit of a cranky teenager at the moment. We have some good times together. 95% I don't know how to answer that. It's been going on a while. I don't like doing it, but maybe it's time to get help. 50%	1. Guilty 40 Angry with self 30 Hopeless 40 2. 30% 20% 50% 3. Tell Kelly I'm sorry about shouting at her and explain why Talk to Viv (my wife) and tell her how I feel instead of shutting her out. Get help?

Combating Self-Critical Thoughts Chart

Date/Time	Situation	Emotions and body sensations Rate each 0–100 for intensity.	Self-critical thoughts Rate each 0–100% for degree of belief.	Alternative perspectives Use the key questions to find other perspectives on yourself. Rate each 0–100% for degree of belief.	Outcome 1. Now that you have found alternatives to your self-critical thoughts, how do you feel (0–100)? 2. How far do you now believe the self-critical thoughts (0–100%)? 3. What can you do (action plan, experiments)?

Combating Self-Critical Thoughts Chart

Date/Time	Situation	Emotions and body sensations Rate each 0–100 for intensity.	Self-critical thoughts Rate each 0–100% for degree of belief.	Alternative perspectives Use the key questions to find other perspectives on yourself. Rate each 0–100% for degree of belief.	Outcome 1. Now that you have found alternatives to your self-critical thoughts, how do you feel (0–100)? 2. How far do you now believe the self-critical thoughts (0–100%)? 3. What can you do (action plan, experiments)?

Combating Self-Critical Thoughts Chart

Date/Time	Situation	Emotions and body sensations Rate each 0–100 for intensity.	Self-critical thoughts Rate each 0–100% for degree of belief.	Alternative perspectives Use the key questions to find other perspectives on yourself. Rate each 0–100% for degree of belief.	Outcome 1. Now that you have found alternatives to your self-critical thoughts, how do you feel (0–100)? 2. How far do you now believe the self-critical thoughts (0–100%)? 3. What can you do (action plan, experiments)?

Combating Self-Critical Thoughts Chart

Date/Time	Situation	Emotions and body sensations Rate each 0–100 for intensity.	Self-critical thoughts Rate each 0–100% for degree of belief.	Alternative perspectives Use the key questions to find other perspectives on yourself. Rate each 0–100% for degree of belief.	Outcome 1. Now that you have found alternatives to your self-critical thoughts, how do you feel (0–100)? 2. How far do you now believe the self-critical thoughts (0–100%)? 3. What can you do (action plan, experiments)?

Combating Self-Critical Thoughts Chart

Date/Time	Situation	Emotions and body sensations Rate each 0–100 for intensity.	Self-critical thoughts Rate each 0–100% for degree of belief.	Alternative perspectives Use the key questions to find other perspectives on yourself. Rate each 0–100% for degree of belief.	Outcome 1. Now that you have found alternatives to your self-critical thoughts, how do you feel (0–100)? 2. How far do you now believe the self-critical thoughts (0–100%)? 3. What can you do (action plan, experiments)?

Combating Self-Critical Thoughts Chart

Date/Time	Situation	Emotions and body sensations Rate each 0–100 for intensity.	Self-critical thoughts Rate each 0–100% for degree of belief.	Alternative perspectives Use the key questions to find other perspectives on yourself. Rate each 0–100% for degree of belief.	Outcome 1. Now that you have found alternatives to your self-critical thoughts, how do you feel (0–100)? 2. How far do you now believe the self-critical thoughts (0–100%)? 3. What can you do (action plan, experiments)?

Combating Self-Critical Thoughts Chart

Date/Time	Situation	Emotions and body sensations Rate each 0–100 for intensity.	Self-critical thoughts Rate each 0–100% for degree of belief.	Alternative perspectives Use the key questions to find other perspectives on yourself. Rate each 0–100% for degree of belief.	Outcome 1. Now that you have found alternatives to your self-critical thoughts, how do you feel (0–100)? 2. How far do you now believe the self-critical thoughts (0–100%)? 3. What can you do (action plan, experiments)?

Key Questions

To Help You Find Alternatives to Self-Critical Thoughts

1   What is the evidence?

- Am I confusing a thought with a fact?

- What is the evidence in favour of what I think about myself?

- What is the evidence against what I think about myself?

2   What alternative perspectives are there?

- Am I assuming my perspective is the only one possible?

- What evidence do I have to support alternative perspectives?

3   What is the effect of thinking the way I do about myself?

- Are these self-critical thoughts helpful to me, or are they getting in my way?

- What perspective might be more helpful to me?

4   What are the biases in my thinking about myself?

- Am I jumping to conclusions?

- Am I using a double standard?

- Am I thinking in all-or-nothing terms?

- Am I condemning myself as a total person on the basis of a single event?

- Am I concentrating on my weaknesses and forgetting my strengths?

- Am I blaming myself for things which are not really my fault?

- Am I expecting myself to be perfect?

5   What can I do?

- How can I put a new, kinder perspective into practice?

- Is there anything I need to do to change the situation? Even if not, what can I do to change my own thinking about it in future?

- How can I experiment with acting in a less self-defeating way?

Outcome

Go back to your original emotions and body sensations. How strong are they now? Rate each one out of 100 per cent for intensity. Then go back to your original self-critical thoughts. Having found alternatives to them, how far do you believe them? Rate each 1 to 100 per cent according to how far you believe it *now*.

If your answers have been effective, you should find that your belief in the self-critical thoughts, together with the painful emotions that go with them, has lessened to some extent.

Now work out what you need to do in order to test out your new perspectives in the real world (this is like checking out your anxious predictions in practice). Experience is the best teacher: you will find your alternatives most convincing if you have acted on them and discovered for yourself how they change your feelings and the possibilities open to you.

Frequently asked questions about the Combating Self-Critical Thoughts Chart

Here are some of the questions people often ask about the **Combating Self-Critical Thoughts Chart**.

How long will it take to find good alternatives to my self-critical thoughts?

The habit of self-criticism takes time to break. Changing your thinking is rather like taking up a new form of exercise. You are being asked to develop mental muscles you do not normally use. They will feel awkward and uncomfortable at first. But, with regular practice, they will become strong, flexible and able to do what you require of them. The objective at this stage is to reach the point where you automatically notice, answer and dismiss self-critical thoughts. Regular daily practice (one or two written examples a day) is the best way to achieve this. You may find it takes you about a week to get the hang of answering self-critical thoughts – or it may take longer.

Later, you will be able to find answers to self-critical thoughts in your head without needing to write anything down. Eventually, you may find that most of the time you do not even need to answer thoughts in your head – they no longer occur very much. Even so, you may still find the record sheet helpful when dealing with particularly tough thoughts, or at times when you are pressurized or unhappy for some reason. But regular daily recordings need only go on until you achieve the objective of dealing with self-critical thoughts without a written prompt.

How can I expect to think differently when I'm feeling really upset?

If something happens that upsets you deeply, it will probably be very difficult to find alternatives to your self-critical thoughts. Instead of grasping that this is a common, natural difficulty, you may fall into the trap of seeing it as yet another reason to criticize yourself. The most helpful thing to do is simply to make a note of what happened to upset you, and your feelings and thoughts, but then to leave the search for alternatives until you are feeling calmer. You will be in a better position to see things clearly after you have weathered the storm.

How good does the record have to be?

Many people with low self-esteem are perfectionists. However, it is important to bear in mind the purpose of the record: increasing self-awareness and increasing flexibility in your thinking. Taking a perfectionist approach won't help you to achieve this – it will only create pressure to perform, and stifle creativity. You do not have to find the one *right* answer, or the answer you think you *should* put. The 'right' answer is the answer that makes sense to you and changes your feelings for the better. No answer, however sensible it may seem, will work for everyone. You need to find the one that works best for *you*.

What if my alternatives don't work?

Sometimes people find that the answers they come up with make little difference to how they feel and act. If this is the case for you, perhaps you are disqualifying the answer in some way – maybe telling yourself that it applies to other people, but not to you? If you have 'yes, buts' like this, write them down in the 'Self-critical thoughts' column and question them. Do not expect your belief in your old thoughts and painful feelings to shrink to zero right away, especially if they reflect beliefs about yourself which have been in place for many years. Self-critical thinking can be like a pair of old shoes – not very pleasant, but familiar and moulded to your shape. New perspectives, in contrast, are like new shoes – unfamiliar and stiff. You will need time to practise 'walking in them' until they start to feel comfortable.

What if I'm no good at this?

Don't allow yourself to get caught in the trap of self-criticism while you are recording your self-critical thoughts. Changing how you think about yourself is no easy task. So beware of being hard on yourself when you find the going tough. If you had a friend who was trying to tackle something difficult, would it be more helpful to praise or to criticize them? You may catch yourself thinking 'I must be really stupid to think this way' or 'I'm not doing enough of this' or 'I will never get the hang of this'. If you do spot thoughts like these – write them down and answer them.

How can you use key questions to help you find alternatives to self-critical thoughts?

The questions summarized on p. 65 and detailed below are designed to help you explore fresh perspectives and recognize how biased and distorted your self-critical thoughts are. At first, you may find it helpful to use the whole list. Then, as you go along, you will notice which questions seem particularly helpful in tackling your own personal style of self-critical thinking. You could write down these especially helpful questions on a card small enough to carry in your wallet or purse, and use them to free up your thinking when self-critical thoughts strike. With practice, useful questions will become part of your mental furniture. At this point, you will no longer need a written prompt.

1 What is the evidence?

Am I confusing a thought with a fact?

Just because you believe something to be true, it does not follow that it is. I could believe that I am a giraffe. But would that make me one? Your self-critical thoughts may be opinions based on unfortunate experiences you have had, not a reflection of your true self.

What is the evidence in favour of what I think about myself?

What are you going on, when you judge yourself critically? What actual evidence do you have to support what you think of yourself? What facts or observations (rather than ideas or opinions) back up your self-critical thoughts?

What is the evidence against what I think about myself?

Can you think of anything that suggests that your poor opinion of yourself is not completely true? Or indeed contradicts it? Finding counter-evidence may not be easy, because you will tend to screen it out or discount it. This does not mean it does not exist.

2 What alternative perspectives are there?

Am I assuming that my perspective on myself is the only one possible?

Any situation can be viewed from many different angles. How would you see this particular situation on a day when you were feeling more confident and on top of things? How do you think you will view it in ten years' time? What would you say if a friend of yours came to you with this problem? If your loss of confidence has been relatively recent, how would you have viewed the situation before the difficulty began?

   Remember to check out alternative perspectives against available evidence. An alternative with no basis in reality will not be helpful to you.

3 What is the effect of thinking the way I do about myself?

Are these self-critical thoughts helpful to me, or are they getting in my way?

What are your goals or objectives in this situation? Right now, do the disadvantages of self-critical thinking outweigh its advantages? Is it the best way to get what you want out of the situation, or would a more balanced, kindly, encouraging perspective be more helpful? Are your self-critical thoughts helping you to handle things constructively, or are they encouraging self-defeating behaviour?

4 What are the biases in my thinking about myself?

Am I jumping to conclusions?

This means deciding how things are, without proper evidence to support your point of view – for example, concluding that the fact that someone didn't call you means that you have done something to offend them, when actually you have no idea why they haven't called. People with low self-esteem typically jump to whatever conclusion reflects badly on themselves. Is this a habit of yours? If so, remember to review the evidence, the facts. When you look at the bigger picture, you may discover that your critical conclusion about yourself is incorrect.

Am I using a double standard?

People with low self-esteem are often much harder on themselves than they would be on anyone else. To find out if you are using a double standard, ask yourself what your reaction would be if someone you cared about came to you with a problem. Would you tell them that they were weak or stupid or pathetic, or that they should know better? Or would you be encouraging and sympathetic and try to help them to get the problem into perspective and look for constructive ways of dealing with it? Try taking a step back from your usual critical and disapproving stance and start being kind, sympathetic and encouraging to yourself, just as you would to another person. You will almost certainly find that this makes you feel better and helps you think clearly and act constructively.

Am I thinking in all-or-nothing terms?

All-or-nothing (or 'black-and-white') thinking oversimplifies things. But nearly everything is relative. So, for example, people are not usually all good or all bad, but a mixture of the two. Events are not usually complete disasters or total successes, but somewhere in the middle. Are you thinking about yourself in black-and-white terms? The words you use may be a clue here. Watch out for extreme words (always/never, everyone/no one, everything/nothing). They may reflect black-and-white thinking. In fact, things are probably less clear-cut than that. So look for the shades of grey.

Am I condemning myself as a total person on the basis of a single event?

People with low self-esteem commonly make global judgements about themselves on the basis of one thing they said or did, or one problem they have. Are you making this kind of blanket judgement about yourself? One person dislikes you, and it must mean there is something wrong with you? One mistake, and you are a failure? Judging yourself as a total person on the basis of any single thing does not make sense. If you did one thing really well, would that make you totally wonderful as a person? You probably wouldn't even dream of thinking so. But when it comes to your weaknesses and mistakes, you may be only too ready to write yourself off.

You need to look at the bigger picture. And remember that when you are feeling down, you will be homing in on anything that fits with your poor opinion of yourself, and screening out anything that does not fit. This biases your judgement even more. So hold back from making global judgements, unless you are sure that you are taking all the evidence into account.

Am I concentrating on my weaknesses and forgetting my strengths?

People with low self-esteem commonly overlook problems they have successfully handled in the past, and forget resources that could help them to overcome current difficulties. Do you tend to focus on things that go wrong, and ignore anything you have enjoyed or achieved?

Of course, there are things you are not very good at, things you have done that you regret, and things about yourself that you would prefer to change. This is true for everyone. But what about the other side of the equation? What are the things you *are* good at? What do other people appreciate about you? What do you like about yourself? How have you coped with difficulties and stresses in your life? What are your strengths, qualities and resources?

Am I blaming myself for things which are not really my fault?

When things go wrong, do you consider all the possible reasons why this might be so, or do you immediately assume that it must be due to some failing in yourself? If a friend stands you up, for example, do you automatically assume that you must have done something to annoy them?

There are all kinds of reasons why things do not work out. Sometimes, of course, it will indeed be a result of something you did. But often, other factors are involved. For example, your friend might have forgotten, or been exceptionally busy, or have misunderstood your arrangements. If you automatically assume responsibility when things go wrong, you will not be in the best position to discover the real reasons for what happened. If a friend of yours was in this situation, how would you explain what had happened? How many possible reasons can you think of? If you remain open-minded and ask yourself what other explanations there might be, you may discover that what happened may have had absolutely nothing to do with you.

Am I expecting myself to be perfect?

It is just not possible to get everything 100 per cent right all the time. If you expect to do so, you are inevitably setting yourself up to fail. Accepting that you aren't perfect means setting realistic targets for yourself, and giving yourself credit when you reach them, even if you haven't achieved perfection. This will encourage you to feel better about yourself, and so motivate you to keep going and try again. It also means that you can learn from your difficulties and mistakes, rather than being upset and even paralysed by them.

5 What can I do?

What can you do to put your new, kinder perspective into practice?

How can you find out if your alternative perspective works better for you? Is there anything you can do to change the situation that sparked the self-critical thoughts (e.g. changing or leaving a job where you are not valued, or ending a relationship with a person who reinforces your negative view of yourself)? Or could you change your own reactions? Old habits die hard – what will you do if in future you find yourself thinking, feeling and acting in the same old way? How would you like to handle the situation differently, next time it occurs?

This will include spotting and dealing with self-critical thoughts. It may also involve experimenting with behaving in new ways that are less self-defeating (e.g. accepting compliments gracefully, not apologizing for yourself, taking opportunities, asserting your own needs, etc.). Write down your ideas on your record sheet, and then take every opportunity to try them out, to develop and strengthen new perspectives on yourself.

Summary

1 Self-critical thoughts are triggered when you sense that experience has confirmed your Bottom Line.

2 Self-critical thinking is a learned habit. It does not necessarily reflect the truth about you.

3 Self-criticism does more harm than good. Believing your self-critical thoughts makes you feel bad and encourages you to act in self-defeating ways.

4 You can learn to stand back from self-critical thoughts – seeing them as something you do, rather than as a reflection of your true self.

5 Self-critical thoughts, like anxious predictions, can be questioned. You can observe them and their impact on your feelings, body state and behaviour, and then search for more balanced and kindly perspectives on yourself.

6 The final step is to experiment with treating yourself less harshly, valuing your strengths, qualities, assets and talents as you would those of another person. This will be the focus of the next section.

SECTION 3: Learning to Accept and Appreciate Your Positive Qualities

In Sections 1 and 2 of this workbook, you learned how to check out anxious predictions and combat self-critical thoughts. These skills are vital in establishing a new, more positive and realistic Bottom Line (central belief about yourself). In Section 3, we shall look at the other side of the coin – becoming more aware of your personal assets and resources, talents and strengths. Changing the negative bias in how you see yourself to a more balanced perspective is not always quick and easy. If you learned to think badly of yourself at an early age, you will not have developed a habit of accepting and appreciating yourself as you are. If this is the case, then be aware that change may take time, be persistent, and keep an open mind, so that you can take advantage of the methods described here to enhance your self-esteem.

This section will help you understand:

- how to develop a balanced view of yourself

- how to identify your good points and positive qualities

- how to make them real

- how to value everyday pleasures and achievements

- how to increase your enjoyment of life

Try this exercise.

How would you react to hearing someone make the following statements?

- 'I'm beautiful'

- 'I'm clever'

- 'I'm a brilliant cook'

- 'I have an excellent sense of humour'

- 'I have great musical talent'

- 'I'm adorable'

- 'I'm great'

Tick your most likely reactions. Would you:

- [ ] **a** Be delighted to meet someone so gifted?

- [ ] **b** Feel uncomfortable and disapproving?

- [ ] **c** Find yourself muttering 'Bighead', or 'Talk about blowing your own trumpet'?

- [ ] **d** Instantly take it for granted that these things must be true?

- [ ] **e** See such statements as boasting, getting above oneself?

- [ ] **f** Feel that it was about time this person was cut down to size?

If you have low self-esteem, you may well have ticked **b**, **c**, **e** and **f**. The idea of allowing yourself to acknowledge your good points may seem to you like boasting. The very thought may make you squirm with embarrassment. You may also fear that, if you admit anything good about yourself, someone else will be sure to step in and say 'Oh, no, you aren't'. Such feelings stand in the way of enhancing self-esteem.

Yet, in fact, it makes no sense to assume that self-acceptance – noticing and taking pleasure in your strengths and qualities and treating yourself like someone who deserves the good things in life – will inevitably lead to smugness and complacency. Clear-eyed, realistic assessment of your strong points is a vital part of self-esteem. Ignoring your positive characteristics helps to keep low self-esteem going, because it stops you from having a balanced view that takes into account the good things about yourself as well as genuine shortcomings and things you might prefer to change.

How can you develop a balanced view of yourself?

If you have low self-esteem, the chances are that you are acutely aware of your mistakes and weaknesses, but very far from accepting and appreciating positive things about yourself. To develop a more balanced view of yourself, it's helpful to begin by making a list of your qualities, talents, skills and strengths. As well as enhancing your self-esteem, this will sharpen your awareness of how you discount and ignore your good points.

As you embark on this task, be on the alert for self-critical thoughts – they are almost certain to pop up when you start to focus on positive qualities. Your aim is to be able to notice these criticisms calmly and let them go without taking them seriously. If you can do so, simply put them to one side and continue with your task. If on the other hand they keep competing for your attention and are hard to dismiss, then write them down on a **Combating Self-Critical Thoughts Chart** (see Section 2, p. 58) and find answers to them before moving on.

> ## It's worth remembering...
>
> **Self-criticism is a habit that will weaken, so long as you keep self-critical thoughts in perspective and refuse to allow them to stop you adopting a more positive view of yourself.**

Some people find making a list of positive qualities quite easy. Their doubts about themselves may be relatively weak, or may surface only in particularly challenging situations. Other people, with very powerful and convincing Bottom Lines, find listing positive qualities almost impossible. The habit of screening them out and discounting them can be so strong that it is difficult at first to accept any good points at all.

You may find that you need some help, perhaps from a close friend or someone else you care about. It is worth spending time on this task. Even if it takes a while to come up with a good list, becoming aware of your positive qualities as part of your everyday life will eventually have a considerable impact on how you feel about yourself.

To get started:

- Choose a time and place where you can be sure you will not be interrupted and settle down with a pen or pencil.

- Make sure you are sitting somewhere comfortable, where you feel peaceful and relaxed. You could perhaps put on some music you enjoy.

- Now, in the box on p. 78, make a list of as many good things about yourself as you can think of. You may be able to list several straight away. Or you may be hard put to think of even one or two. You can use the questions below to help you if you wish.

- Give yourself plenty of time, and don't worry if the task is hard at first. You are trying something new, finding a fresh perspective on yourself.

- Take your list as far as you can, and when you feel you have come up with as many items as possible for the time being, stop.

- Put this workbook somewhere easily accessible – it may even be helpful to carry it with you. Over the next few days, even if you are not actually working on your list, keep it at the back of your mind and add to it as things occur to you.

- Be pleased even if you can find only one or two things to begin with. You have made a good start in freeing up your thinking and taken the first crucial step towards acknowledging and accepting good things about yourself.

My Good Points (qualities, talents, skills, strengths)

How can you identify your good points and positive qualities?

If your self-esteem has been low for some time, you will almost certainly have difficulty in identifying your strong points and positive qualities. This does not mean that you do not have any – it just means that you are out of the habit of noticing and appreciating them. Here are some questions to help you.

Key Questions

To Help You Identify Your Good Points

1 What do you like about yourself, however small and fleeting?

2 What positive qualities do you possess?

3 What have you achieved in your life, however small?

4 What challenges have you faced in your life?

5 What gifts or talents do you have, however modest?

6 What skills have you acquired?

7 What do other people like or value in you?

8 What qualities and actions that you value in others do you share?

9 What aspects of yourself would you appreciate if they were aspects of another person?

10 What small positives are you discounting?

11 What are the bad qualities you do *not* have?

12 How might another person who cared about you describe you?

---

1 What do you like about yourself, however small and fleeting?

- Look out for anything about yourself that you have ever felt able to appreciate, even if only momentarily.

2 What positive qualities do you possess?

- Include qualities that you feel you do not possess 100 per cent, or that you do not show all the time.

- Give yourself credit for having the quality at all, rather than discounting it because you have it to a less than perfect extent.

3 What have you achieved in your life, however small?

- You are not looking for anything earth-shattering here – like winning the Olympics, or being the first to cross the Sahara on a donkey.

- Take into account small steps you have successfully achieved.

4 What challenges have you faced in your life?

- What anxieties and problems have you tried to conquer?

- What difficulties have you dealt with?

- What qualities in you do these efforts reflect?

- Facing challenges and anxieties takes courage and persistence, whether or not you resolve them successfully. Give yourself credit for this.

5 What gifts or talents do you have, however modest?

- What do you do well? (Take note: 'well', not 'perfectly'!)

- Again, remember to include the small things. You do not need to be Michelangelo or Beethoven. If you can boil an egg, or whistle a tune, or make someone laugh, then add it to the list.

6 What skills have you acquired?

- What do you know how to do? Include work skills, domestic skills, people skills, academic skills, sporting skills and leisure skills.

- For example, do you know how to use a telephone, a computer, a microwave or a saw?

- Can you catch a ball? Can you drive a car or ride a bicycle? Do you know how to swim, how to sew or how to clean a bathroom?

- Are you good at listening to people, or appreciating their jokes? Can you read in a thoughtful way? Have you learned any languages?

- Think about all the different areas of your life and note down skills you have in all of them, however partial or basic.

7 What do other people like or value in you?

- What do they thank you for, ask you to do, or compliment you on?

- What do they praise or appreciate?

- You may not have been paying much attention to this. Now is the time to start.

8 What qualities and actions that you value in other people do you share?

- It may be easier for you to see other people's strong points than your own. Which positive qualities that you appreciate in others do you also possess?

- Beware of unfavourable comparisons here. You do not have to be or do whatever it is to the same degree as the other person. You just need to acknowledge that you share the quality, even if only to a limited extent.

9 What aspects of yourself would you appreciate if they were aspects of another person?

- If there are aspects of yourself that you would appreciate if they were another person's, write them on your list.

- Think also about things you do that you would appreciate and value if another person did them.

- Write down anything that you would count as a positive if it were done by someone else.

10 What small positives are you discounting?

- You may feel that you should only include major positives on your list. But would you discount small negatives in the same way?

- If not, write the small positives down. Otherwise it will be impossible to achieve a balanced view.

11 *What are the bad qualities you do not have?*

- Think of some bad qualities (e.g. 'irresponsible', 'cruel' or 'dishonest'). Is this how you would describe yourself?

- If your answer is 'no', then you must be something else. What is it (e.g. 'responsible', 'kind' or 'honest')?

- Write down the mirror images of the bad qualities you identified. Again, don't discount the good qualities because you don't think you possess them to a great enough extent.

12 *How might another person who cared about you describe you?*

- Think about someone you know who cares about you, respects you and is on your side. They may have a more balanced view of you than you have of yourself.

- What sort of person would they say you were? What words or phrases would they use to describe you? How would they see you as a friend, a parent, a colleague or a member of your community?

- If there is someone close to you, whom you respect and trust, ask them to make a list of the things they like and value in you. Choose someone you have good reason to believe cares about you and wishes you well (e.g. a parent, a brother or sister, a partner, a child, a friend or a colleague with whom you have a close relationship). You may find their list a very pleasant surprise, and it will strengthen your relationship.

- Again, watch out for thoughts that lead you to discount and devalue what you read (for example, that they are only doing it to be kind and can't possibly mean what they say). If you have thoughts like these, write them down and answer them on a **Combating Self-Critical Thoughts Chart** (see Section 2, p. 58).

CASE STUDY: Sarah

Sarah, the artist described in Part One of the course whose parents had never been able to appreciate her talent, had some difficulty with her list, as you might imagine. Experience had taught her to place very little value on herself, and in particular to devalue what to other people appeared a striking gift. At first, she could not think of anything to write except 'good-natured' and 'hard-working'. Trying to add other items roused all sorts of reservations (e.g. 'But other people are better at that than me' or 'But that isn't really important').

After a couple of tries, she used the questions on p. 79 to free up her thinking. She still found it hard but eventually added 'thoughtful', 'practical', 'good colour sense', 'persistent', 'creative', 'kind', 'good taste', 'adventurous cook' and 'open to new ideas'. In addition, she screwed up her courage and asked an old and trusted friend if he would make a list of her good points too. He said it was about time she gave her confidence a boost, and set to with a will. Sarah was moved and delighted by the affection that shone through his list. He echoed some of the items on her own list, and added 'makes me laugh', 'good listener', 'good drinking companion', 'has created a welcoming home', 'intelligent', 'sensitive' and 'warm'.

How can you make your good points and positive qualities real?

Give yourself a few days to notice more items to add to your list and then, when you feel you have taken it as far as you can for the time being, once again find yourself a comfortable, relaxing spot and read the list to yourself.

Pause and dwell on each good point and quality you have recorded, and let it sink in. When you have read slowly and carefully through the list, go back to the top again. Now, as you consider each item, bring to mind a particular time when you showed that quality in how you behaved. Take time to make the memory as clear and vivid as you can. Close your eyes, and recall it in detail – almost as if you were living it again:

- When was it?

- Where were you?

- Who were you with?

- What exactly did you do that showed the positive quality in action?

- What were the consequences (what did you notice, how did you feel, how did others react, and so on)?

Notice what effect this exercise has on your mood and how you feel about yourself. If you can absorb yourself in it fully, recreating what happened in your mind's eye and calling up the feelings you had at the time, you will find that the items on your list become much more vivid and meaningful to you. You should find your mood lifting, and you may begin to notice a growing sense of self-acceptance and confidence.

If this does not happen, look out for feelings of shame, embarrassment or disbelief. These feelings may indicate the presence of self-critical thoughts. Are you, for example, telling yourself that it is wrong to be so smug? Do you feel as if you are showing off? Are you thinking that what you did was trivial – anyone could have done it? Are you telling yourself that you could have done it better? Or faster? Or more effectively? Or are you devaluing your qualities because you think they are too ordinary to be worth considering?

When disclaimers like these intrude, simply notice their presence and then go back to focusing fully on your list of positive qualities. If the disclaimers are too strong to be ignored, you can combat them, using the skills you learned for dealing with self-critical thoughts in Section 2 (pp. 56–72).

Keeping a Good Points Chart

The next step is to make this awareness of your positive qualities an everyday event by recording examples of your good points every day, as they occur, just as you previously recorded examples of anxious predictions and self-critical thoughts. Your objective is to reach the point where you automatically notice good things that you do, without needing to write them down. You may reach this point in three or four weeks, or it may take longer. Once you get there, there is no further need for the chart.

Use your list of qualities, skills, strengths and talents as a prompt to help you get started and keep a copy of your **Good Points Chart** with you, so that you can write things down as soon as they happen. Otherwise, examples may be missed, forgotten or discounted. Decide in advance how many examples of positive qualities you wish to record every day. Many people find that three is about right to start with. If this seems to be too many, however, then don't be afraid to start with two, or even one. Wherever you start, as you get into the swing of it, you will be able to add more. When recording three incidents is easy, increase the number to four. When four is easy, go up to five, and so on. By then, noticing pluses should be pretty automatic.

For each entry on the chart, write down the date and time, a description of what you did, and what positive quality it showed. Make sure that what you did is described in enough detail for you to remember what it was when you look back on it, e.g. 'helped old Mrs Jackson cross the road with her shopping', not 'was kind'.

On the opposite page is an example of a **Good Points Chart** filled in by Sarah.

On pages 86–88 you will find **Good Points Charts** for you to fill in, and two other blank charts at the back of the workbook, which you can photocopy if you wish.

Good Points Chart: Sarah

Date/Time	What I did	Positive quality
12 March morning	Spent several hours completing a large landscape painting	Hard-working
12 March evening	Went out with Simon. Haven't laughed so much in ages	Good drinking companion, funny
13 March afternoon	Bought flowers	Creating a welcoming home
13 March evening	Tried cooking a Thai curry for the first time – tasted odd, but was edible	Adventurous cook
14 March morning	Called Mother as it was her birthday	Kind
14 March afternoon	Fixed shelving in workroom	Practical

Good Points Chart

Date/Time	What I did	Positive quality

Good Points Chart

Date/Time	What I did	Positive quality

Good Points Chart

Date/Time	What I did	Positive quality

At the end of each day, perhaps just before you go to bed, make time to relax and be comfortable and review what you have recorded. Look over what you have written, and recreate the memory of what you did in vivid detail. Let it sink in, so that it affects your feelings and your sense of yourself. You can also review your charts at the end of the week, to get an overview, and to decide how many examples of good points to look out for the following week. They will become a store of pleasurable, confidence-building memories that you can call on any time you are feeling stressed, low or bad about yourself.

How can you learn to value everyday pleasures and achievements?

If you have low self-esteem, you may miss out on everyday pleasures and achievements because you do not take the trouble to make your life enjoyable (perhaps you feel you don't deserve it?), or give yourself credit for what you do. This is especially likely to be true when you are feeling down or depressed.

The first step towards learning to value your everyday experiences is to get a clear picture of how you spend your time, how satisfying your pattern of daily activities is to you, and how good you are at acknowledging your achievements and successes.

Keeping a Daily Activity Diary

The **Daily Activity Diary (DAD)** is one way of getting the information you need. You will find an example filled in by Sarah on pp. 90–1.

The diary looks a bit like a school timetable, with the days across the top and the times down the left-hand side – but don't let that put you off! It will give you a real insight into how you spend your time and a basis for finding a pattern of activity that really works for you. Each day is divided into hourly slots, in which you can record what you do and what you gain from what you do. This means noting how much you enjoy your activities and how far you give yourself credit for your achievements.

The **DAD** can help you to:

- keep an accurate record of your everyday experiences, as they happen

- identify changes you would like to make in how you spend your time

- focus on positive aspects of your experience

- spot 'killjoy thoughts' that lead you to discount and disqualify your pleasures and successes

Daily Activity Diary: Sarah

	Time	Monday	Tuesday	Wednesday	Thursday	Friday	Saturday	Sunday
MORNING	6–7				Sleep	Sleep	Sleep	Sleep
	7–8				"	" / M0 P3	"	"
	8–9				" / M0 P5	Got up; coffee; shower M3 P2	" / M0 P5	" / M0 P5
	9–10				Got up; breakfast; radio M1 P4	Out to buy art materials	" / M0 P5	Got up – tired; breakfast; shower M5 P2
	10–11				Worked M2 P4	" M3 P4	Got up; breakfast; shower M2 P4	Worked M5 P2
	11–12				" M2 P6	Coffee with M. M0 P6	Drove out to Henley M3 P4	" M4 P5
	12–1				" M1 P6	Worked M6 P3	Lunch with cousins M1 P6	" M4 P5
AFTERNOON	1–2			Met agent for L. wants me to exhibit M5 P0	Lunch in park M0 P6	" M6 P5	"	Lunch with J. M0 P6
	2–3			" M4 P1	Cleaned up mess in apartment M7 P0	" M4 P7	"	" M0 P8
	3–4			Went round to see F. M0 P1	" M8 P0	Called agent and agreed to exhibit M10 P2	Walked along the river by myself M2 P5	Went to the zoo with J. M0 P8
	4–5			M0 P5	Sat & read M1 P4	Worked M4 P6	M3 P5	"

EVENING

	Monday	Tuesday	Wednesday	Thursday	Friday	Saturday	Sunday
5–6			*Worked M6 P3*	*Shopping M2 P3*	*" M4 P6*	*" M8 P3*	*Home M0 P2*
6–7			*" M4 P6*	*met J. & F. for drinks & eats M1 P6*	*" M3 P1*	*Drove home M3 P2*	*Worked M2 P4*
7–8			*Supper M1 P4*	*Theatre M0 P10*	*Supper M1 P4*	*Phoned Mum M4 P1*	*" M5 P2*
8–9			*P. came round depressed M4 P2*	*"*	*TV M0 P6*	*Listened to music, thinking about work*	*" M3 P4*
9–10			*" M4 P4*	*"*	*" M0 P8*	*" M0 P6*	*" M2 P6*
10–11			*Read M0 P6*	*Pub again M0 P8*	*" M0 P1*	*Met P. for late drink M1 P7*	*Bed M0 P5*
11–12			*Bed M0 P4*	*Back to J's apartment M0 P8*	*Bed M0 P4*	*"*	*"*
12–1			*"*	*"*	*"*	*Bed M0 P8!*	*"*

Review: (What do you notice about your day? What worked for you? What did not work? What would you like to change?)

Mon:

Tues:

Weds: *Didn't enjoy lunch at all. He was hassling me. As usual, couldn't believe anyone would really like my work.*

Thurs: *Some good work, which I enjoyed. Great evening – worth planning more of this.*

Fri: *Hard to get started on work, but sticking with it paid off. Called agent and said yes – terrifying but I need to do it. Treated myself to relaxed, mindless evening at home.*

Sat: *Walk a good idea but too long. Should have paced myself.*

Sun: *Planned lunch w. J a great success. Lot of fun watching street theatre in Covent Garden.*

Over the course of a week or so, keep a detailed daily record of your activities, hour by hour. You will gather the most useful information if the week you record is typical of your life at the moment. This is the information that will be most helpful when you come to consider changes you wish to make. If you record your activities over an exceptional week (e.g. you were on holiday, you were off sick, or your mother had come to stay), the information you gather will only really be directly relevant to similar times in the future, not to your everyday life.

Each hour, write down:

What you did

Simply note the activity (or activities) you were engaged in. Anything you do counts as an activity, including sleeping and doing nothing in particular. Even 'doing nothing' is actually doing something. What does it mean exactly? Sitting, staring into space? Pottering around, doing minor domestic tasks? Sitting slumped on the couch, channel-surfing?

Rating of Pleasure (P)

How much did you enjoy what you did? Give each activity a rating between 0 and 10. 'P10' would mean you enjoyed it very, very much. Sarah, for example, gave 'P10' to Thursday's evening at the theatre with friends. She felt she had thoroughly enjoyed herself. The play was excellent, funny and thought-provoking, and she had had a really good time with people she knew very well and felt completely relaxed with. 'P5' would mean moderate enjoyment. So, for example, Sarah gave 'P5' to Saturday's walk in the country by herself. She had enjoyed the warmth of the sunny day, but had miscalculated the distance, so that she was very tired by the time she got back to her car. 'P0' would mean you did not enjoy an activity at all. Sarah gave 'P0' to Wednesday's meeting with her agent, who was hassling her to exhibit her recent paintings – even though normally she would have enjoyed his company as she liked and respected him.

You can use any number between 0 and 10 to show how much you enjoyed a particular activity. Like Sarah, you will probably find that your pleasure level varies, according to what you do. This variation will be a useful source of information. It shows what works for you, and what does not work. It may give you clues about killjoy thoughts that get in the way of satisfaction and enjoyment. (For example, Sarah was aware that she could not enjoy talking to her agent because she was preoccupied with fears about exposing her work to public view.)

Rating of Mastery (M)

How far was each activity an achievement, a mastery experience? 'M10' would mean a very considerable achievement. Sarah gave herself 'M10' for the phone call she made to her agent on Friday. This was because she called to agree that she would submit work to an exhibition, despite her anxieties. She gave herself a high 'M' rating as recognition that this was a difficult thing to do, and she had to push herself, but she did it. 'M5' would mean a moderate achievement. Sarah gave herself 'M5' on Sunday morning when she got up in time to complete a picture she was working on, despite still feeling tired from her walk. Her first reaction was that getting up was nothing special, but she realized on reflection that, given how tired she felt, it was quite an achievement. 'M0' would mean no sort of achievement at all. Sarah gave herself 'M0' for an evening at home watching television. This was pure self-indulgence, and she enjoyed it, but it did not involve any sort of achievement and so she felt happy to give it a 0 for 'M'.

Again, like Sarah, you could use any number between 0 and 10 to judge how much mastery you experienced carrying out a particular activity.

It is important to realize that 'mastery' does not only refer to major achievements like getting a promotion, hosting a party for 100 guests, or spring-cleaning the whole house from top to bottom. Everyday activities can be real achievements, for which you deserve to give yourself credit. This is especially the case if you are feeling stressed, tired, unwell or depressed. When you are not in a good state emotionally, even relatively minor routine activities (answering the telephone, making a snack, getting to work on time, even getting out of bed) can represent substantial achievements. Not recognizing this often leads people with low self-esteem to devalue what they do and, of course, this helps to keep low self-esteem going.

So when you rate 'M', remember to take into account how you felt at the time. Ask yourself: 'How much of an achievement was this activity, *given how I felt at the time?*' If carrying out the activity represents a triumph over feeling bad, a real effort, a difficulty confronted, then you deserve to give yourself credit for it, even if it was routine, not done to your usual standard, or not completed.

Make sure that you rate all your activities for both P and M. Some activities (e.g. duties, obligations, tasks) are mainly M activities. Some are mainly P (relaxing and pleasurable things that we do just for ourselves). Many activities are a mixture of the two. For example, going to a party might warrant a good M rating if socializing makes you anxious, because it represents a triumph over your negative predictions. But once you arrived and began to relax and have a good time, the party could become enjoyable, too. In the long run, you are aiming for a balance of M and P. Giving both ratings to all your activities will help you to achieve this.

Review

At the end of each day, take a few minutes to look back over your diary. A brief daily review will encourage you to reflect on what you have done, rather than simply writing it down and leaving it.

- What do you notice about your day?
- What does the record tell you about how you are spending your time, and how much pleasure and satisfaction you get from what you do?
- What worked for you?
- What did not work?
- What were the high points, both in terms of pleasure and of mastery?
- What were the low points?
- What would you like more of or less of?
- What would you like to change?

Now is your chance to fill in your own **Daily Activity Diary**. You will find copies on pp. 96–103 and more blank diary sheets, which you can photocopy if you wish, on pp. 116–23. The first four are for recording what you do now, as we have just described. The rest are for the next step: planning your day so as to maximize your enjoyment and satisfaction in what you do.

Frequently asked questions about filling in the Daily Activity Diary

Here are some questions people often ask about the Daily Activity Diary (DAD).

How long should I carry on keeping the record?

The objective of the record is to give you a clear idea of how you are spending your time, and how pleasurable and satisfying your daily activities are to you. The record is also an opportunity to start noticing how negative thinking patterns (e.g. self-critical thoughts and anxious predictions) may prevent you from making the most of your experiences. So continue the record until you feel you have enough information for these objectives to be met. For many people, a week or two is enough. But if you feel you need more time to observe yourself, then there is no need to stop at that point.

When should I complete the record sheet?

It is important to record what you did, and your ratings, *at the time*, whenever possible. In the course of a busy day, things are easily forgotten. In addition, negative biases are likely to give you a clear memory of things that did not go well, and to screen out pleasures, successes and achievements (especially if you are feeling generally low and bad about yourself). Noting your activities and ratings *at the time will* help to counter this bias. Immediate ratings also help you to tune into even small degrees of pleasure and mastery that may otherwise go unnoticed. Finally, if you put off recording what you do, you are more likely to forget to do it, put it off until tomorrow, or perhaps give up altogether before you have collected the information you need.

If for some practical reason it is difficult for you to carry your chart with you, then record what you do somewhere else – your diary, for example, another sheet of paper, or even the back of an envelope. You can transfer the information to your chart later.

What if I discover that I am not enjoying anything very much?

This could be because you are not making space in your day for enjoyable activities. You can use the **DAD** to check whether this is so. Perhaps you do not feel you deserve to enjoy yourself. Or perhaps you feel uncomfortable about putting yourself first, or taking time out just to relax. If you suspect that this may be the case, look carefully at the pattern of your day. What proportion of time is given over to activities that are relaxing, pleasurable, fun and just for you? If your day is filled with tasks, obligations, duties and things you do with other people in mind, then increasing enjoyable activities may be one of your objectives at the next stage.

On the other hand, maybe you are engaging in activities that should be pleasurable, but killjoy thoughts are preventing you from enjoying them fully. Look for examples in your record of activities that should have been enjoyable, but in fact were not. Ask yourself:

- What was going on while you were engaging in them?
- Were you fully absorbed in what you were doing? Or were you actually preoccupied with other things?
- Were you making comparisons with other people, who seem to be enjoying themselves more than you?
- Were you making comparisons with how things used to be at some time in the past, or with how you think things *should* be?

(Frequently asked questions continues on p. 104.)

Daily Activity Diary

	Monday	Tuesday	Wednesday	Thursday	Friday	Saturday	Sunday
MORNING							
6–7							
7–8							
8–9							
9–10							
10–11							
11–12							
AFTERNOON							
12–1							
1–2							
2–3							
3–4							
4–5							

	Monday	Tuesday	Wednesday	Thursday	Friday	Saturday	Sunday
5–6							
6–7							
7–8							
8–9							
9–10							
10–11							
11–12							
12–1							

EVENING

Review: (What do you notice about your day? What worked for you? What did not work? What would you like to change?)

Mon:

Tues:

Weds:

Thurs:

Fri:

Sat:

Sun:

Daily Activity Diary

	Monday	Tuesday	Wednesday	Thursday	Friday	Saturday	Sunday
6–7							
7–8							
8–9							
9–10							
10–11							
11–12							
12–1							
1–2							
2–3							
3–4							
4–5							

MORNING

AFTERNOON

	Monday	Tuesday	Wednesday	Thursday	Friday	Saturday	Sunday
5–6							
6–7							
7–8							
8–9							
9–10							
10–11							
11–12							
12–1							

E V E N I N G

Review: (What do you notice about your day? What worked for you? What did not work? What would you like to change?)

Mon:

Tues:

Weds:

Thurs:

Fri:

Sat:

Sun:

Daily Activity Diary

	Monday	Tuesday	Wednesday	Thursday	Friday	Saturday	Sunday
MORNING 6–7							
7–8							
8–9							
9–10							
10–11							
11–12							
12–1							
AFTERNOON 1–2							
2–3							
3–4							
4–5							

	Monday	Tuesday	Wednesday	Thursday	Friday	Saturday	Sunday
5–6							
6–7							
7–8							
8–9							
9–10							
10–11							
11–12							
12–1							

EVENING

Review: (What do you notice about your day? What worked for you? What did not work? What would you like to change?)

Mon:

Tues:

Weds:

Thurs:

Fri:

Sat:

Sun:

Daily Activity Diary

		Monday	Tuesday	Wednesday	Thursday	Friday	Saturday	Sunday
MORNING	6–7							
	7–8							
	8–9							
	9–10							
	10–11							
	11–12							
AFTERNOON	12–1							
	1–2							
	2–3							
	3–4							
	4–5							

	Monday	Tuesday	Wednesday	Thursday	Friday	Saturday	Sunday
5–6							
6–7							
7–8							
8–9							
9–10							
10–11							
11–12							
12–1							

EVENING

Review: (What do you notice about your day? What worked for you? What did not work? What would you like to change?)

Mon:

Tues:

Weds:

Thurs:

Fri:

Sat:

Sun:

If, when you engage in potentially pleasurable activities, your mind is actually elsewhere, then you will not enjoy them. So watch out for killjoy thoughts and, if you can, simply put them to one side ('Ah, there you are again!') and focus on what you are doing. If they are too strong to put to one side, then write them down and look for alternatives to them (just as you did with anxious predictions and self-critical thoughts).

There is one other possibility. If you find that you are not really enjoying anything at all as you used to, look back at the signs of depression described on p. x. If this picture fits you, you may need to seek treatment for depression in its own right.

What if I'm not achieving anything?

If this appears to be the case, use your record to find out more about what is going on. Perhaps anxious predictions and self-critical thoughts are leading you to restrict your field of activities.

- Do you miss opportunities, for example out of anxiety that you will not be able to cope with them?

- Do you avoid social contacts, in case you make a fool of yourself, or people reject you?

- Do you avoid challenges, convinced that you will not be able to meet them?

If so, then continuing to work on your anxious and self-critical thoughts should help you extend your range of activities, which will allow you to gain a more positive view of your capabilities and enhance your sense of achievement.

If on the other hand you already engage in a wide range of activities, including some that are quite difficult or challenging, perhaps you are allowing self-critical thinking to undermine your sense of achievement. Self-critical thinking reduces motivation and gives a false impression that you are achieving nothing. It may well be based on very high standards you have for yourself (your Rules for Living). Perhaps these prevent you from acknowledging small successes because you think they are not special enough, or should have been done better or faster or more completely?

Watch what runs through your mind when you complete a task. Do your thoughts make you feel good and motivate you to do more? Or do they demoralize and discourage you and leave you feeling you did not do very well and there's little point in continuing? If so, you need to write them down and tackle them, using the skills you have already acquired. Treating yourself more kindly, giving yourself credit, and encouraging yourself will take you further than downgrading what you do and putting yourself down.

How can you increase your enjoyment of life?

Once you have seen how you spend your time, the next step is to introduce changes that will increase your enjoyment, enhance your sense of mastery and achievement, and so help you to feel better about yourself.

Your daily review of your diary should already have given you some idea of the changes you might like to make. Now you can start planning ahead, so as to create a balance between *Mastery* activities (duties, challenges, obligations, tasks) and *Pleasure* activities (relaxation, enjoyment).

As a starting point, think about what you are going to do today – or tomorrow, if this is evening time.

1 _____

2 _____

3 _____

Then write down three activities that might give you a sense of achievement, for example, tasks that you have been putting off or avoiding (*Mastery*):

1 _____

2 _____

3 _____

Now decide how to fit these activities into your day. When exactly will you do each of them, and for how long? Write this down alongside each activity.

Planning your day

In order to plan each day systematically, using the **DAD**s at the back of the book on p. 116–23, you will need to:

Write down your plan for the day

You may prefer to do this first thing in the morning, or in the evening. Choose whichever time is likely to be easiest for you. For example, if your morning is usually madly busy, you could do without the extra task. Use the evening (perhaps when you are relaxing just before going to bed) instead. If, on the other hand, you are normally too tired in the evening to think straight, but usually wake feeling refreshed, then use the morning. You can write your plan in pencil on the **DAD** itself, if you wish, or on the back of the sheet, or on a completely separate piece of paper.

Each day, aim for a balance between *Pleasure* and *Mastery*. If you fill your time with duties and chores, and allow no time for enjoyment, you may end up tired and resentful. On the other hand, if you completely ignore things you have to do, you may find your enjoyment soured by a sense that nothing has been achieved, and the list of tasks you are putting off will keep worrying you.

Record what you actually do

Use your plan as a guide for the day, and write down what you actually do on the **DAD**. If you wrote your plan down in pencil, write what you actually did in a different colour so that it is easy to see which is which. Rate each activity from 0 to 10 for *Pleasure* and *Mastery*, just as you did at the self-observation stage.

> ### *Review your day*
>
> At the end of each day, take a few minutes to sit down comfortably, relax, and review what you have done. Thoughtfully examine how you spent your time:
>
> - How far did you stick to your plan?
> - If you did not, why was that?
> - Did you get sidetracked?
> - Did something come up that you had not predicted?
> - Had you planned too much to start with?

- How much enjoyment and satisfaction did you get from what you did?
- How good was your balance between *Pleasure* and *Mastery*?
- What would you like more of or less of?
- What would you like to change?

Once you get the hang of planning ahead, you may well find that you are automatically looking after yourself by balancing out *Mastery* and *Pleasure* without needing to write anything down. However, a written plan may still be helpful at times in the future, e.g. when you are feeling low and finding it difficult to motivate yourself, or when you are under pressure and need to be reminded that being busy doesn't have to exclude all pleasure and relaxation.

Frequently asked questions about planning ahead

Here are some questions people often ask about planning the day so as to maximize *Pleasure* and *Mastery*.

What if my plan is a success?

Success means devising a realistic plan, with a good balance of pleasurable activities and achievements, accomplishing what you set out to do, and getting the enjoyment and sense of mastery you wanted. If your plan works for you in this way, you have something really positive to build on. You have clearly found a pattern to the day which works well for you, and which you will want to repeat.

However, even if your plan is generally successful, you may still find it helpful to carry out some fine-tuning. For example, you might want to add some regular exercise, or some quality time with your family. Or you might decide to contact someone you have lost touch with, or to tackle a particular task you have been putting off.

What if my plan is a failure?

Plans fail to work out for many reasons. In fact, if your plan 'fails', this is likely to be very useful, because it may tell you why your pattern of activity is not working for you.

Supposing, for example, you planned to spend an evening at the cinema with a friend, but then a colleague persuaded you to work late instead. Or supposing you planned to spend a whole morning catching up with a pile of post, but somehow you never got round to it.

In situations like these, where things do not work out as planned, you could ask yourself:

- What exactly was the problem?

- Did you overestimate what you could do in a particular chunk of time?

- Did you plan too much and exhaust yourself?

- Did you spend the day doing things you felt you *ought* to do, rather than things you would enjoy?

- Did you forget to include time for yourself or for relaxation?

- Or did you fritter away your time on nothing in particular and end up feeling you had had a wasted day?

- Did you end up doing what everyone else wanted, rather than what would have been good for you?

When you have identified the problem, ask yourself:

- Is this pattern familiar to you?

- Are there other situations in which you act in the same way?

- Could what went wrong with your plan reflect a more general rule or strategy of yours?

Once you understand the problem, you can begin to tackle it, by making practical changes and by identifying and questioning the self-defeating thoughts that are keeping you stuck. You may well find that what kept you from fulfilling your plan also gets in your way in other areas of your life.

What if I can't think of anything pleasurable to do?

It may be helpful to treat this difficulty as a special project: how many ways to enjoy yourself can you think of? Write down a list containing whatever comes to mind, however unlikely, without criticizing or censoring it. You can work out the practicalities later. You can use the ideas below to help you, if you wish.

You could start by noticing what other people do for pleasure.

- What about your friends, and other people you know? What about what you see in the media?

_____

_____

_____

_____

_____

_____

- What about all the activities on the noticeboard in your local library and college of further education?

_____

_____

_____

_____

_____

_____

- What do you notice people enjoying when you are out and about?

_____

_____

_____

_____

_____

_____

_____

Then think about yourself, and add to your list.

- Even if you are not doing much for pleasure right now, have there been times in the past when you enjoyed certain activities? What were they?

_____

_____

_____

_____

_____

_____

_____

_____

- Is there anything you have always fancied doing, but never got around to?

_____

_____

_____

_____

_____

_____

- What are all the possible things you could do, even if you have never tried them?

_____

_____

_____

_____

_____

_____

Think of all the different pleasurable activities that might work for you under different circumstances.

- What could you do alone (e.g. reading, watching TV, going for walks)?

_____

_____

_____

_____

_____

_____

- What could you do with other people (e.g. going to the pub, joining an evening class, going to an art gallery)?

_____

_____

_____

_____

_____

_____

- What can you do that takes time (e.g. holidays, day trips, going to stay with people)?

_____

_____

_____

_____

_____

_____

- What can you do that can be easily fitted into the corners of your day (e.g. having a cup of special tea or a glass of special beer, soaking in a hot scented bath, pausing to glance out of the window)?

_____

_____

_____

_____

_____

_____

- What can you do that costs money (e.g. buying some flowers, going to the cinema, having a meal out)?

_____

_____

_____

_____

_____

_____

- What can you do that is free (e.g. looking at a sunset, window-shopping, looking through old photographs)?

_____

_____

_____

_____

_____

_____

- What physical pleasures can you think of (e.g. going swimming, flying a kite, having a massage)?

_____

_____

_____

_____

_____

_____

- What pleasures can you think of that use your mind (e.g. listening to a debate, doing a jigsaw or a crossword)?

_____

_____

_____

_____

_____

_____

- What can you do out of doors (e.g. taking care of your garden, going to the beach, going for a drive)?

_____

_____

_____

_____

_____

_____

● And what can you do at home (e.g. choosing clothes from a catalogue, listening to music, playing computer games)?

_____

_____

_____

Add all these things to your list.

Once you have a list of potential pleasures, plan them into your day. You may still have doubts about whether they will work for you. There is only one way to find out! And remember to watch out for killjoy thoughts. Put them to one side, if you can, and write them down and answer them if they persist in getting in your way. When you give yourself pleasures like these, you are treating yourself like someone you love and care about. This is exactly the approach you need to take to enhance your self-esteem. So look after yourself. You deserve it.

How can I deal with the fact that my day is genuinely full of obligations?

If your day is genuinely very busy, it can be difficult to make time for pleasure and relaxation. It may seem impossible even to fit in one more small thing. However, it is very important to realize that failing to make time just for yourself can backfire on you. You may find that you become increasingly tired and stressed so that, in the end, you are no longer able to do all the things you have to do as well as you would like to. Your health may even be affected. So finding time for relaxation is crucially important to your well-being and that of people around you.

If you take the view that you are entitled to relaxation and pleasure, and that you deserve to care for yourself as you might care for another person, you will be better able to make room for small pleasures, even on very busy days. Think of them as rewards for all your efforts, to which you are fully entitled. Make five minutes for a cup of coffee and a short walk. Take ten minutes for a shower with special soap. Choose something to eat for supper that you really like. Buy a small bunch of flowers that does not cost much. Listen to a favourite programme on the radio while you fix the car. Take advantage of your baby falling asleep to sit and read a magazine instead of feeling obliged to catch up with the housework. Be ingenious and creative, and don't allow yourself to be ground down by a relentless round of tasks and obligations. In the long run, you will not do yourself or anyone else any good.

How can I tackle all the things I have been putting off?

If you have been putting things off for a while, the prospect of facing them may seem rather daunting. However, tackling practical problems will enhance your sense of competence and so help to strengthen your self-esteem. By the same token, avoiding problems and tasks is likely to make you feel less in control of your life, and that will make you feel worse about yourself.

Follow these steps:

- Make a list of the tasks you have been putting off and problems you have been avoiding, in whatever order they occur to you.

- If you can, number the items on the list in order of importance. Which needs to be done first? And then what? And then what? If you cannot decide, or if it genuinely doesn't matter, simply number them in alphabetical order, or as they have occurred to you.

- Take the first task or problem on the list. Break it down into small, manageable steps. Rehearse the steps in your mind. As you do so, write down any practical problems you might encounter at each step, and work out what to do about them. This may involve asking for help or advice, or getting more information.

- As you rehearse what you plan to do, watch out for thoughts that make it difficult for you to problem-solve or tackle the task. You may find anxious predictions coming up (e.g. 'You won't be able to find a solution' or 'You'll never get everything done'). Or you may find yourself being self-critical (e.g. 'You should have dealt with this weeks ago' or 'You are a lazy slob'). If this happens, write your thoughts down and look for more helpful alternatives to them, as you have already learned to do.

- Once you have a step-by-step plan you feel reasonably confident of, tackle the task or problem one step at a time and deal with any practical difficulties and anxious or self-critical thoughts as they occur – just as you did in your rehearsal.

- Write down the end result on your **Daily Activity Diary**, and give yourself ratings for *Pleasure* and *Mastery*. Remember that even a small task completed, or a minor problem solved, deserves a pat on the back, if you have been putting it off!

- Take the next task on the list, and tackle it in the same way.

Daily Activity Diary

	Monday	Tuesday	Wednesday	Thursday	Friday	Saturday	Sunday
6–7							
7–8							
8–9							
9–10							
10–11							
11–12							
12–1							
1–2							
2–3							
3–4							
4–5							

MORNING

AFTERNOON

	Monday	Tuesday	Wednesday	Thursday	Friday	Saturday	Sunday
5–6							
6–7							
7–8							
8–9							
9–10							
10–11							
11–12							
12–1							

EVENING

Review: (What do you notice about your day? What worked for you? What did not work? What would you like to change?)

Mon:

Tues:

Weds:

Thurs:

Fri:

Sat:

Sun:

Daily Activity Diary

		Monday	Tuesday	Wednesday	Thursday	Friday	Saturday	Sunday
M	6–7							
O	7–8							
R	8–9							
N	9–10							
I	10–11							
N	11–12							
G	12–1							
A	1–2							
F	2–3							
T	3–4							
E R N O O N	4–5							

	Monday	Tuesday	Wednesday	Thursday	Friday	Saturday	Sunday
5–6							
6–7							
7–8							
8–9							
9–10							
10–11							
11–12							
12–1							

EVENING

Review: (What do you notice about your day? What worked for you? What did not work? What would you like to change?)

Mon:

Tues:

Weds:

Thurs:

Fri:

Sat:

Sun:

Daily Activity Diary

		Monday	Tuesday	Wednesday	Thursday	Friday	Saturday	Sunday
M O R N I N G	6–7							
	7–8							
	8–9							
	9–10							
	10–11							
	11–12							
A F T E R N O O N	12–1							
	1–2							
	2–3							
	3–4							
	4–5							

	Monday	Tuesday	Wednesday	Thursday	Friday	Saturday	Sunday
5–6							
6–7							
7–8							
8–9							
9–10							
10–11							
11–12							
12–1							

EVENING

Review: (What do you notice about your day? What worked for you? What did not work? What would you like to change?)

Mon:

Tues:

Weds:

Thurs:

Fri:

Sat:

Sun:

Daily Activity Diary

	Monday	Tuesday	Wednesday	Thursday	Friday	Saturday	Sunday
6–7							
7–8							
8–9							
9–10							
10–11							
11–12							
12–1							
1–2							
2–3							
3–4							
4–5							

MORNING

AFTERNOON

	Monday	Tuesday	Wednesday	Thursday	Friday	Saturday	Sunday
5–6							
6–7							
7–8							
8–9							
9–10							
10–11							
11–12							
12–1							

EVENING

Review: (What do you notice about your day? What worked for you? What did not work? What would you like to change?)

Mon:

Tues:

Weds:

Thurs:

Fri:

Sat:

Sun:

Summary

1 To enhance your self-esteem, you need to focus attention on your strong points and on the good things in your life, as well as tackling anxious predictions and self-critical thoughts.

2 Ignoring your strong points and downgrading your achievements and pleasures are part of the bias against yourself that keeps low self-esteem going.

3 You can combat the negative bias by listing your qualities, skills, talents and strengths and noting examples of these in your daily life (the **Good Points Chart**).

4 You can also use a **Daily Activity Diary** to observe how you are spending your time and how much pleasure and satisfaction you get from what you do.

5 These observations will help you start to accept and appreciate your good points and positive qualities, and to make the most of everyday pleasures and achievements.

Extra Charts and Worksheets

Predictions and Precautions Chart

Date/Time	Situation What were you doing when you began to feel anxious?	Emotions and body sensations (e.g. anxious, panicky, tense, heart racing). Rate 0–100 for intensity.	Anxious predictions What exactly was going through your mind when you began to feel anxious (e.g. thoughts in words, images)? Rate 0–100% for degree of belief.	Precautions What did you do to stop your predictions coming true (e.g. avoid the situation, safety-seeking behaviours)?

Questioning Anxious Predictions Chart

Date/Time	Situation	Emotions and body sensations Rate 0–100% for intensity.	Anxious predictions Rate belief 0–100%.	Alternative perspectives Use the key questions to find other views of the situation. Rate belief 0–100%.	Outcome 1. How do you now feel (emotions, body sensations)? 2. How far do you now believe your original predictions (0–100%)?

Using Experiments to Check Out Anxious Predictions Chart

Date/Time	Situation	Anxious predictions Rate belief 0–100%.	Experiment What will I do instead of taking precautions?	Results 1. What have you learned? 2. Were your predictions correct? If not, what perspective would make better sense?

Spotting Self-Critical Thoughts Chart

Date/Time	Situation What were you doing when you began to feel bad about yourself?	Emotions and body sensations (e.g. sad, angry, guilty). Rate each 0–100 for intensity.	Self-critical thoughts What exactly was going through your mind when you began to feel bad about yourself (e.g. thoughts in words, images, meanings)? Rate each 0–100% for degree of belief.	Self-defeating behaviour What did you do as a consequence of your self-critical thoughts?

Combating Self-Critical Thoughts Chart

Date/Time	Situation	Emotions and body sensations Rate each 0–100 for intensity.	Self-critical thoughts Rate each 0–100% for degree of belief.	Alternative perspectives Use the key questions to find other perspectives on yourself. Rate each 0–100% for degree of belief.	Outcome 1. Now that you have found alternatives to your self-critical thoughts, how do you feel (0–100)? 2. How far do you now believe the self-critical thoughts (0–100%)? 3. What can you do (action plan, experiments)?

Good Points Chart

Date/Time	What I did	Positive quality

Good Points Chart

Date/Time	What I did	Positive quality

Thoughts and Reflections

Thoughts and Reflections